RECLAIMING
C.A.L.M

A Practical Guide to Managing Anxiety

WHITNEY COLEMAN, LICSW, LCSW-C

Jade Clinical Services LLC
Whitney Coleman, LICSW, LCSW-C

Printed Worldwide
First Printing 2025
First Edition 2025

10 9 8 7 6 5 4 3 2 1

Interior Book Design by Walt's Book Design
www.waltsbookdesign.com

Published by: Jade Clinical Services LLC
www.jadeclinical.com

RECLAIMING
C.A.L.M

TABLE OF CONTENTS

DEAR READER

This book is personal to me in a way that goes beyond the usual work of a professional clinician. Yes, I come to you as a mental health professional, but I also come to you as someone who has lived inside the skin of anxiety for as long as I can remember.

I know what it feels like to have a panic attack in a crowded room, to feel shamed when anxiety hijacks a simple moment, to be told I was just "melodramatic" or "high strung." I know what it feels like to carry that weight quietly (or sometimes loudly), fearing I was the only one who couldn't just "calm down."

Long before I had language for what was happening, I had to figure out how to survive it. I built tools before I even knew they had names, experimenting with ways to soothe myself when the world felt too sharp, too fast, too much. Later, as I grew into my professional role, I began learning the science that explained what my body and mind already knew - and I realized I wasn't alone, and neither are you.

So, this book is both lived and learned. It comes from nights I thought would never end and days I thought I'd never get through. It comes from the conversations I've had with people who, like you and me, were just trying to breathe without shame, to steady themselves without feeling misunderstood or ignored.

If you've ever felt unseen in your anxiety, if you've ever carried the sting of being dismissed or misunderstood, please know: I see you here. This space is for you. I wrote these pages so you wouldn't have to keep figuring it out alone.

May you feel less isolated, more understood, and a little lighter as you turn these pages. Together, we can reclaim calm - not as perfection, not as the absence of anxiety, but as a steadier, kinder way of moving through the world.

With warmth and solidarity,

Whitney

INTRODUCTION

WHY THIS BOOK EXISTS

If you're reading this, anxiety has likely been your unwelcome companion for some time now. Perhaps you've kept it hidden, carrying it like a secret weight. Or maybe it's written all over your face, impossible to disguise. You might find yourself pushing through endless workdays, caring for family members, juggling countless responsibilities—all while trying to hold everything together as your thoughts race faster than you can possibly catch them.

You're here because you're exhausted from letting anxiety call the shots. Maybe you've already tried the usual suspects: meditation apps, therapy sessions, self-help articles. Nothing quite clicked. Nothing truly stuck. I understand completely, and that's precisely why this book exists.

Over the years, I've sat across from countless individuals who describe feeling overwhelmed, jumpy, restless, or completely stuck in place. I've witnessed intelligent, compassionate people berate themselves for not being "calm enough" or "together enough." Through all these conversations, I've discovered something crucial: **the way we typically talk about anxiety often makes it significantly worse.**

Think about the advice you've probably heard: "Just calm down." "Stop overthinking." "Don't worry about it so much." These well-meaning suggestions treat anxiety like a light switch you can simply flip off at will. When you inevitably can't make that switch work, it's easy to feel like you're failing at the basic task of being "normal."

Here's the foundational truth I want you to carry with you throughout this journey: **anxiety is not a character flaw.** It's not evidence that you're weak, damaged, or somehow lagging behind everyone else. Anxiety is actually your brain's sophisticated alarm system saying, "I've detected something that might be threatening, and I'm working overtime to keep you safe." That response? Completely, utterly human.

The real problem arises when that internal alarm system gets jammed in the "on" position. Suddenly, everyday life begins to feel like an relentless, high-stakes exam you never agreed to take, where the pressure never lets up and the stakes always feel impossibly high.

This book won't attempt to "fix" you—because you don't need fixing. You're not broken. Instead, this book will teach you how to **work alongside** your anxiety rather than exhausting yourself fighting it at every turn. We'll explore a straightforward, compassionate approach that I use in my practice every single day. I call it **CALM**.

- **Comfort**: Remind yourself you're not alone.
- **Anchor**: Ground in safety and the present moment.
- **Look (at it differently):** See the situation in a kinder, more helpful way.
- **Move (it forward)**: Take one small step toward relief.

You can read straight through or skip to what you need right now. Either way, you'll get tools, stories, and prompts that help you understand your anxiety and respond to it differently - *today*, not someday.

What This Book Is (and Isn't)

This book is:

- A friendly guide you can use in real life.
- A place to practice skills that actually fit your day.
- A set of tiny steps that stack up.

This book isn't:

- A test you can fail.
- A lecture packed with big words.
- A promise that you'll never feel anxious again.

You'll have anxious moments again because you're human. But you'll have a plan. And that changes everything.

Why Anxiety Shows Up So Loud

Deep within your mind lives an ancient guardian—a neural alarm system designed to keep you alive. Thousands of years ago, this hypervigilant protector served our ancestors well, scanning the horizon for predators and shouting "Run!" when genuine threats appeared.

That same alarm system still operates within you today, but it hasn't quite caught up with modern life. Your brain can't always distinguish between a saber-toothed tiger and a difficult conversation with your boss. Both trigger the same primal response: *Danger ahead!*

Meet CALM: Your Four-Step Friend

Think of CALM like a pocket plan you can use anywhere. You don't have to do all four steps every time. One step can help. Use what fits.

Comfort

Talk to yourself like you would talk to someone you love.

- "This feeling is hard, and I'm still okay."
- "Lots of people feel this before a big moment."
- "I can be kind to myself right now."

Anchor

Help your body feel safe in the present.

- Place both feet on the floor.
- Inhale 4, hold 2, exhale 6.
- Notice one color you see, one sound you hear, one sensation you feel.

Look (at it differently)

Shift the story in your head.

- "Is there another way to see this?"
- "What would I say to a friend in my shoes?"
- "What facts do I have? What's guesswork?"

Move (forward)

Take one small, doable step.

- Send one email.
- Drink a glass of water.
- Write three words you need to remember.
- Step outside for two minutes of fresh air.

Baby steps count. Baby steps are how big change begins.

How to Use This Book

Use it your way. Here are a few ideas:

- **Read in order** if you want a steady path.
- **Skip around** if a chapter calls your name.
- **Try the exercises** as you go. You don't need perfect answers.

- **Use a notebook** or your phone to jot quick notes.
- **Keep a "CALM card."** Write the four steps on an index card or in your notes app. Pull it out when anxiety spikes.

A gentle rhythm that helps:

1. Read a few pages.
2. Try a tool for one minute.
3. Write one sentence about what you noticed.
4. Keep the parts that help. Leave the rest.

How CALM Works in Real Life

Let's walk through a few common moments. Use the lines in quotes if you like.

The Meeting Spiral

You've got a big presentation in ten minutes, and your heart is racing.

- **Comfort:** "Lots of people feel this before speaking."
- **Anchor:** Feel your feet. Feel the chair. Three slow breaths.
- **Look:** "This energy can help me stay alert."
- **Move:** Open your slides. Star your top three points.

The 2 A.M. What-Ifs

You wake up, and your mind starts racing about tomorrow.

- **Comfort:** "My brain is trying to help me prepare."
- **Anchor:** Notice the texture of your pillow. Listen for the softest sound in the room.
- **Look:** "These are thoughts, not facts. I can look at them tomorrow."

- **Move:** Jot down a quick note for the morning. Listen to a meditation or calming music.

The Social Overload

You're at a gathering, and it all feels too loud.

- **Comfort:** "It's okay to need a break."
- **Anchor:** Step outside. Feel the air on your face. Breathe out longer than you breathe in.
- **Look:** "I can enjoy this in small moments, not all at once."
- **Move:** Choose a time to re-enter, or head home.

The Inbox Flood

You open your email, and there are 47 unread messages.

- **Comfort:** "Anyone would feel stressed seeing this."
- **Anchor:** Hands on your desk. One slow breath in, longer breath out.
- **Look:** "Not everything needs me right now."
- **Move:** Sort by **Today**, star 3, answer 1.

The Waiting Room

You're waiting for results or an appointment, and your chest feels tight.

- **Comfort:** "Waiting is hard. I'm not alone."
- **Anchor:** Box breathing—In 4, hold 4, out 4, hold 4 (repeat).
- **Look:** "I can't control the outcome, but I can care for myself now."
- **Move:** Sip water. Text one steady person: "Thinking of me helps."

Your Starter Agreements (So You Don't Fight Yourself)

- **Small counts.** One breath, one kind word, one baby step.
- **No shaming.** Talk to yourself like someone you love - if you say something negative or critical, try again.
- **Curiosity over judgment.** Ask "What's happening?" not "What's wrong with me?"
- **Bodies talk.** If your body whispers, listen early.
- **Rest is allowed.** You can pause and still be strong.

Set Your Starting Point

Grab a notebook or your notes app. Answer in quick, honest lines. No essays needed.

- Today, my anxiety feels like ___ (color, weather, sound).
- Three places I feel a little safer are ___.
- My go-to comforts are ___.
- Early signs my anxiety is rising: ___.
- One person I can text for support is ___.
- One tiny move I can do most days: ___.

Snap a photo of your answers. They're your map.

Your Starting Questions

Take a few minutes with these. Be honest - this isn't a test and no one needs to see it.

- What made you want to work on your anxiety right now?
- What have you already tried?
- How would you describe your relationship with anxiety - constant, occasional, or something else?

- What do you want to get out of this book?
- Do you believe your anxiety is valid? Why or why not?
- How do you usually react when you feel anxious - push through, avoid, ask for help, or something else?
- What support do you already have? (Friends, routines, coping tools)
- What would "feeling better" look like for you?
- How do you want to talk to yourself when you're anxious?
- How can CALM be your guide?

Some answers may come fast. Some may feel tender. Every answer is a piece of your map forward.

How to Get the Most From This Book

- **Pick one chapter** to practice each week.
- **Choose one CALM step** per day to focus on.
- **Track your tiny wins.** Write one line each night: "Today I...."
- **Circle back** to any chapter when life shifts.
- **Ask for more help** if you need it. Therapy, support groups, and trusted people can sit beside you while you practice.

What You Can Expect as You Practice

You'll still have anxious days. But over time you may notice:

- You catch spirals earlier.
- Your body settles a little faster.
- Your self-talk gets kinder.
- You feel less stuck and more willing to try.

That's progress. That's your nervous system learning it can trust you.

Where We're Going Next

We'll start by getting clear on what anxiety really is and what it's not. We'll look at how your brain and body talk to each other. We'll slow down anxious thoughts and try new words that fit better. We'll map your triggers, build routines, and practice the four steps in everyday life.

You don't have to do it perfectly. You just have to keep showing up for yourself, one small step at a time. I'll walk with you.

Ready? Let's begin.

CHAPTER ONE

UNDERSTANDING ANXIETY

If we're going to work **with** anxiety instead of fighting it, we need to get clear on what it is, how it works, and how it shows up in daily life. People use the word a lot—before a test, during a job search, walking into a room full of strangers. Those are pieces of anxiety, but not the whole story.

Here's the big idea we'll use all through this book: **anxiety is a safety mechanism.** It is your body and brain trying to protect you. That system is helpful when there's real danger. It's draining when the alarm gets stuck on.

This chapter gives you a simple map. It's written so anyone can use it, so go ahead and use it.

A Working Definition

Anxiety is a body–brain response to a **real or perceived** threat.

It includes:

- **Thoughts** (worry, "what-ifs," fear of the future)
- **Feelings** (uneasy, tense, on edge)
- **Body sensations** (racing heart, tight chest, shaky hands)
- **Actions** (avoid, over-prepare, seek reassurance, freeze)

You are not "broken" if you feel anxious. You are human.

Anxiety as an Alarm System

Think of anxiety like a smoke detector.

- **When there's a fire:** You want the alarm to be loud. It keeps you safe.
- **When there's toast burning:** The alarm still goes off. It's annoying, but there's no real danger.

If your inner alarm is **very sensitive**, it may ring:

- At the wrong time (false alarm)
- For too long (keeps blaring after the threat is gone)

The goal of this book: Teach your alarm to be **accurate** and **shorter**, not silent. We want a right-sized alarm.

What Anxiety *Is* and What It *Isn't*

Anxiety IS

- A normal human response
- Your brain's "pay attention" signal
- A mix of thoughts, feelings, body cues, and actions
- Your mind and body trying to protect you

Anxiety IS NOT

- Proof you're weak
- A character flaw
- Something you can switch off by willpower alone
- Always bad (sometimes it helps you prepare and perform)

When you treat anxiety as a **messenger** instead of an **enemy**, you respond with skill instead of shame.

Why We Have Anxiety

Long ago, humans survived by spotting danger fast.

- Hear a rustle → body gets ready to **fight, run, or hide**.

- Hormones like adrenaline help you move and focus.
- This response is fast and automatic.

Today, the same system turns on for:

- Job interviews
- First dates
- Public speaking
- Uncertain news
- A phone buzz after a hard conversation

The **problem** isn't that we have anxiety. The problem is that modern life sends **many** "maybe" threats. The alarm gets a lot of action.

How Anxiety Show Can Up (Three Lenses)

1) Body Signs

- Racing heart
- Tight chest or throat
- Shaky hands or legs
- Sweaty palms
- Stomach flips, nausea, bathroom urges
- Headaches, jaw clenching, tense shoulders
- "Can't catch my breath" feeling

2) Feeling Signs

- Dread or fear
- Irritable, snappy
- Restless or wired-tired
- Overwhelmed, "too much"
- Numb or disconnected

3) Behavior Signs

- Avoiding people or tasks
- Over-preparing, checking again and again
- Asking for reassurance a lot
- Keeping super busy to outrun worry
- Freezing - your mind goes blank, can't act

Note: Many people call these behaviors "stress," "perfectionism," or "being a planner." It may still be anxiety. Naming it gives you choices.

Quick Self-Check: The SUDS Scale

Use the **SUDS** (Subjective Units of Distress Scale) to rate your anxiety from **0 to 10**.

- **0–2:** Calm or slightly tense
- **3–4:** Noticeable worry, still functioning
- **5–6:** Uncomfortable, hard to focus
- **7–8:** Very anxious, urge to escape
- **9–10:** Panic-level, overwhelmed

This is *not* a diagnosis tool. It's a **tracking tool**. It helps you see patterns and pick the right skill at the right time.

The Four Threat Responses

When your alarm rings, you may shift into one of these:

- **Fight:** Push back, argue, get sharp or intense
- **Flight:** Leave, avoid, change plans fast
- **Freeze:** Mind goes blank, body feels stuck
- **Fawn:** Please others to feel safe, say "yes" when you mean "not now"

You might have a favorite, or you may switch based on the situation. Noticing your pattern is step one.

The Anxiety Cycle

Anxiety often runs the same loop:

1. **Trigger**

- Something eternal (a look, an email) or internal (a thought, a memory) sets it off.

2. **Body Reaction**

- Heart races, stomach flips, muscles tense.

3. **Scary Thoughts**

- "I can't handle this." "Something bad is coming."

4. **Safety Behaviors**

- Avoid, over-check, over-prepare, or seek reassurance.

5. **Temporary Relief**

- You feel better for a bit.

6. **Learning (by your brain)**

- "Aha - avoiding helped." So the next time, the alarm rings **sooner** and **louder**.

Good news: You can break this loop by changing **any one** step - body, thoughts, or actions.

Evidence-Informed Micro-Skills (Plain Language)

- **Slow out-breath** lengthens the "calm" part of your nervous system.

- **Grounding your senses** pulls you into the here-and-now.
- **Labels for thoughts** ("I'm having the thought that…") create space.
- **Tiny actions** retrain your alarm that "this is safe enough."

Simple doesn't mean weak. Simple is **trainable**.

CALM in Practice (Preview)

We'll use CALM again and again. Here's how it maps onto the cycle:

- **Comfort** (meets shame): "My alarm is loud because it cares."
- **Anchor** (meets body): Plant feet, breathe slow, orient to the room.
- **Look** (meets thoughts): "Is there another way to see this?"
- **Move** (meets behavior): One small step that points toward what matters.

You don't need perfect conditions. You need a place to start.

Case Examples

The Meeting Spiral

Ten minutes before presenting, your chest is tight.

- Comfort: "Nerves mean I care."
- Anchor: Feet on floor, exhale longer than inhale (4–6).
- Look: "I know my top three points."
- Move: Open slides; say the first sentence out loud.

The 2 A.M. What-Ifs

Wide awake, mind racing.

- Comfort: "My brain is trying to protect me."

- Anchor: Feel the blanket; listen for the quietest sound.
- Look: "These are thoughts, not facts. Morning-me will decide."
- Move: Write one line on a note; press play on a calming track.

Social Overload

Party gets loud; you feel flooded.

- Comfort: "It's okay to take space."
- Anchor: Step outside; cool air on face.
- Look: "I can take this in small chunks."
- Move: Choose a return time - or leave on purpose.

Map Your Pattern

My early body signs:

_____

Common triggers:

_____

My usual safety behaviors:

_____

One kinder thought I can practice (Comfort/Look):

_____

One tiny action I can try next time (Move):

_____

Take a photo of your answers. That's your pocket plan.

Language That Lowers the Alarm

Swap harsh lines for gentler ones:

- From "What's wrong with me?" → **"What's happening in me?"**
- From "Stop it, calm down!" → **"Slow down, I'm here."**
- From "I can't handle this." → **"I can handle the next 60 seconds."**
- From "It must be perfect." → **"It can be good enough to start."**

Words shape your nervous system. Choose ones that help.

When to Get Extra Support

Reach out to a professional if you notice:

- Panic attacks that keep returning
- Anxiety that prevents sleep, school, caregiving, or work
- Constant worry plus sadness, hopelessness, or thoughts of self-harm
- Using alcohol or substances to shut off the alarm

Getting help is a **strength move**, not a failure.

Why This Matters

When you understand anxiety, you stop treating yourself like a problem. You start working with your wiring. You learn to:

- Catch the cycle sooner
- Lower the body alarm
- Pick kinder thoughts
- Take small steps that build confidence

You don't have to erase anxiety to live well. You need tools that make it the **right-size** for the situation.

Quick Tools You Can Use Today

1-Minute Anchor

- Inhale through your nose for 4
- Hold for 2
- Exhale through your mouth for 6
- Repeat 4 times

Name 3–2–1

- 3 things you see
- 2 things you feel (touch)
- 1 sound you hear

10% Move

- Shrink a task to 10%: one paragraph, one email, one phone call. Do that. Done counts.

Myths vs. Facts

Myth: Strong people don't feel anxious.

Fact: Strong people **work with** anxiety.

Myth: If I avoid this, I'll feel better.

Fact: You'll feel better **now**, and more anxious **next time**.

Myth: Anxiety means danger.

Fact: Anxiety means **possible** danger—or a false alarm.

Putting It Together: A Simple Flow

1. **Notice**: "My alarm is ringing."
2. **Name**: Rate it 0–10.

3. **Nervous system first**: One Anchor.
4. **Thought check**: One Look line.
5. **Action**: One Move that matches your values.
6. **Log a win**: "I used CALM at a 6/10."

Rinse and repeat. Skill grows with reps.

15 Questions to Reflect On

Answer in a notebook, a voice memo, or just in your head. There are no wrong answers, only honest ones.

1. How do you define anxiety in your own words?
2. What does your anxiety feel like in your body?
3. When did you first notice anxiety in your life?
4. What triggers your anxiety most often?
5. Do you try to avoid anxiety or push through it?
6. Have you ever felt ashamed about your anxiety?
7. What situations or people increase your anxiety?
8. How do you typically react when anxiety shows up?
9. What would it mean to "normalize" your anxiety?
10. How has anxiety protected you in the past?
11. What messages about anxiety did you get growing up?
12. Do you feel safe when you're anxious?
13. Can you name any unhelpful beliefs you hold about anxiety?
14. What would moving forward with anxiety, not without it, look like?
15. Which part of CALM do you already use without realizing it?

Key Takeaway

Anxiety isn't the enemy. It's a **messenger**. Your work isn't to silence it forever. Your work is to **listen, right-size the alarm**, and **respond** in ways that keep **you** in charge.

Next, we'll go deeper into **Comfort**, the first step of CALM - so you can stop treating anxiety like a personal failure and start meeting it with care.

CHAPTER TWO

THE BRAIN-BODY CONNECTION

Anxiety isn't just "in your head." It lives in your whole body. Your brain and body talk all day long. When anxiety shows up, that chat turns into ALL CAPS. So, let's slow it down a tad. When you understand what's happening inside you, anxiety feels less like a monster under the bed and more like a loud alarm that needs guidance.

This chapter gives you both: the science in plain words and the skills you can use right away. You can read it like an everyday guide, and you can also use it as a teaching tool with kids, or teams, or clients.

A Simple Map of Your Nervous System

Think of your nervous system like a car with **a gas pedal and a brake**.

- **Gas (go system):** Speeds you up so you can act. This is your **fight/flight** energy.
- **Brake (rest system):** Slows you down so you can think, digest, and sleep.
- **Emergency brake:** When things feel too much, your body may **freeze** or **shut down** for a bit to protect you.

Your goal isn't to always be calm. Your goal is to **shift gears on purpose** - speed up when you need to, slow down when you can.

What Happens in Your Brain When You're Anxious

Let's walk through it in simple steps:

1. **Amygdala (the security guard):**

- This tiny, almond-shaped part scans for danger. If it sees a threat (real **or** possible), it hits the alarm.

2. **Hypothalamus (the command center):**

- Gets the alert and sends messages to the body: "Get ready!"

3. **Stress hormones:**

- Adrenaline and cortisol move fast through your body. They help you act. You may notice:
  - Faster heartbeat
  - Tight muscles
  - Quick, shallow breathing
  - Sharper senses (the world around you feels louder and brighter)

4. **Thinking brain goes dim for a moment:**

- The part of your brain that plans, reasons, and chooses words (your prefrontal cortex) gets less power when the alarm is loud. This is why it's hard to "just think positive" in the middle of a surge. You're not weak, your brain is doing its job.

Here's the tricky part: your guard can't always tell the difference between **real danger** and **maybe danger**. So the same body rush can happen when a dog barks **and** when your boss says, "Can we talk?"

Fight, Flight, Fawn, and Freeze

You may lean toward one or two of these. You might also switch based on the situation.

Fight (push back):

- Snappy tone, tight jaw, urge to argue or control.

- *Helps:* unclench jaw, lengthen exhale, lower voice on purpose, loosen hands.

Flight (get away):

- Avoid, cancel, leave early, scroll to escape.
- *Helps:* plant feet, name 3 things you see, take 10 slow steps while counting.

Freeze (stuck):

- Blank mind, heavy body, can't decide.
- *Helps:* gentle movement (roll shoulders, wiggle toes), cold water on wrists, one simple choice: "Stand… or sit."

Fawn (please to feel safe):

- Say yes when you mean not now, over-apologize.
- *Helps:* hand on chest, one boundary sentence ready: "Let me get back to you."

None of these mean you're broken. They mean your system is trying to keep you safe.

How Chronic Anxiety Affects the Body

The alarm is meant for short bursts. When it stays on for weeks or months, you may feel worn down. You might notice:

- Muscle tension, jaw pain, or headaches
- Tired but wired (hard to fall or stay asleep)
- Upset stomach, reflux, or bathroom changes
- Chest tightness or short breath feeling
- Low energy, brain fog
- Getting sick more often

It's like driving with your foot on the gas all day. The engine runs hot. We're going to help you use the **brake** more often and sooner.

Spot the Early Signs (Catch It Small)

Your body often whispers before it shouts. Early signs can show up hours, or days, before a spike:

- Shoulders creeping up toward your ears
- Jaw clenching or teeth grinding
- A pit or tightness in your stomach
- Fast heartbeat or shallow breath
- Trouble focusing, zoning out
- Restless energy, pacing, picking at skin
- Feeling both tired **and** revved up

Try this: Rate your tension right now on a 0-10 scale. Jot it down. Do one of the grounding tools below. Rate again. That's your data.

Anchor Skills: Breath, Body Awareness, and Rhythm

Your brain needs proof that you're safe. Your body can send that proof fast.

1) Breath (lengthen your exhale)

Your breath is a remote control for your nervous system.

- Inhale **4** (nose)
- Hold **2**
- Exhale **6** (mouth, like blowing through a straw)
- Repeat 5-7 times

Tips if breath work spikes your anxiety:

- Focus only on the **longer exhale**.
- Count out loud.
- Hum on the exhale. Vibration calms the body.
- Try a **physiological sigh**: small inhale + bigger inhale + long exhale.

2) Body Awareness (come back to the room)

Anchor your attention in the present.

- Feel your hands on your legs; press down and release.
- Notice the weight of your hands on your legs.
- Find three colors you can see right now.
- Name: one thing you see, one thing you hear, one thing you feel.

3) Rhythm (steady movement)

Repetitive motion settles the system.

- Gentle walk; count steps 1-20, repeat
- Rocking in a chair or swaying while standing
- Tapping left-right on thighs (bilateral tapping)
- Slow shoulder rolls; stretch hands wide, then soft

Why it works: Your body tells your brain, "We're safe enough to move slowly." The alarm softens.

Build Your "Anchor Kit"

Make a small kit you can use at home, work, or on the go.

- A smooth stone, stress ball, or textured fabric
- Earbuds with a calming playlist

- Mints or gum (taste anchors you)
- A note card with your breath count and one kind sentence
- Lavender or citrus scent stick (if scents help you)

Keep one in your bag, one on your desk, one by your bed.

A Daily Body Plan (Morning, Midday, Night)

Morning (2-5 minutes)

- Reach arms overhead, then fold forward and let head hang
- Two rounds of 4-2-6 breathing
- One sentence to self: "Today I will go slower than my worry."

Midday (1-3 minutes)

- Stand, shake out hands, roll ankles
- Name 3 objects by color (blue, green, red)
- Drink water; long exhale for 6 counts

Evening (5 minutes)

- Put phone away for the last 10-30 minutes
- Hand on chest, one gentle check-in: "What do I need?"
- Progressive release: tighten shoulders 5 seconds, release; repeat head to toe

Tiny doses, many times, beat one long session once a week.

When Panic Hits (A Short Plan)

1. **Name it:** "This is a panic surge. It will pass."
2. **Ground:** Feel the wall with your palm; describe its temperature and texture.

3. **Breathe out long:** 4-6 count exhale, or sighs.
4. **Move a little:** Walk 10 slow steps; count them.
5. **Reset thought:** "My body can ride this wave."
6. **Aftercare:** Water. Protein snack. Short rest if you can.

You're not trying to "stop" the wave. You're surfing it with skill.

Gentle Science, Plain Words

- **Sympathetic system** = gas pedal (fight/flight).
- **Parasympathetic system** = brake (rest/digest).
- Long exhales and steady movement invite the **brake**.
- Safety cues (soft voice, warm face, friendly touch if welcome) invite the brake too.

You don't have to remember the terms. You only need the **shifts**.

Everyday Examples

The unexpected email

- Body first: feet on floor, one slow exhale.
- Then brain: "I can read, then respond. Not everything is urgent."

School pickup traffic

- Body first: count 5 things you see outside the car.
- Then brain: "I'm safe in this seat. We'll get there."

Medical waiting room

- Body first: cold water on wrists, 4-2-6 breathing.
- Then brain: "I can handle the next 10 minutes."

Tracking What Works (A Mini-Log)

- **Trigger/Setting:** _____
- **Body signs (0–10):** _____
- **Anchor used:** _____
- **After rating (0–10):** _____
- **Note to self:** _____

Two lines. That's it. After a week, you'll see patterns.

Common Roadblocks (and Workarounds)

- **"Breathing makes me dizzy."**
- Try long exhales only. Or hum. Or count steps instead. **"I forget the tools."**
- Put sticky notes where your eyes land: mirror, laptop, steering wheel (parked).
- **"I feel silly."**
- Private first. Bathroom stall, parked car, walk around the block.
- **"It works, then I stop."**
- Pair it with something you already do (habit stacking): after brushing teeth → 3 slow breaths.

10 Questions to Reflect On

Take your time. Short answers are great.

1. Where in your body do you carry stress?
2. What physical symptoms scare you most?
3. How does your body respond when you're anxious?
4. How long does it take your body to calm down after a stressful event?

5. Do you notice any patterns between your thoughts and your body?
6. What do you currently do to feel physically calm?
7. What types of movement or touch bring you comfort?
8. Have you ever ignored physical symptoms of anxiety?
9. How can you use your body to send your brain a message of safety?
10. What would it look like to make peace with your body instead of battling it?

Try This Now (2 Minutes)

- Sit back. Drop your shoulders.
- Exhale slowly for 6 counts.
- Name one thing your body did well today (walked you here, hugged someone, carried groceries).
- Whisper: "Thank you, body."
- Notice any shift, even 1%.

The Main Thing to Hold

Your body is **not** your enemy. Anxiety is your body trying to protect you, even when it overreacts. When you listen for early signs and use anchors, breath, body awareness, and rhythm, you send a clear message back up to your brain:

We're safe enough right now. We can think. We can choose.

That's control you can feel.

CHAPTER THREE

REFRAMING ANXIOUS THOUGHTS

If anxiety had a soundtrack, it wouldn't be soft piano. It would be that one song that loops and won't quit-the lyrics are your worries, fears, and "what-ifs."

Sometimes the volume is low, and you barely notice it. Other times it blares so loud you can't think about anything else. It feels real. Your body reacts. That's why these thoughts are so convincing.

So, let's slow the track down. We'll look at what anxious thinking sounds like, why your brain returns to it, and how to **rewrite the story** with skills you can use any day.

What Anxious Thinking Sounds Like

Anxious thoughts have a "flavor." You'll hear common openers:

- **"What if…"**
- "What if I mess this up?" "What if I get sick?" "What if they laugh at me?"
- **"I can't…"**
- "I can't handle this." "I can't go." "I can't do it without panicking."
- **"They must think…"**
- "They must think I'm boring." "They must think I'm unqualified."
- **"It's going to…"**
- "It's going to be a disaster." "It's going to go wrong."

You might also notice **quiet versions**:

- The inner narrator that only points out what went wrong.
- The quick flash of fear when a text says, "Can we talk?"
- The voice that turns a small mistake into a full identity: "I'm a failure."

These thoughts feel true because your **body joins in** (fast heart, tight chest), and your body's reaction makes the thought seem even more true. That loop is strong, but it's trainable.

Why Your Brain Falls for These Thoughts

Your brain loves patterns. If a thought shows up often, the brain marks it as a "favorite" and offers it again, like **autoplay for worry**. The brain also leans toward "better safe than sorry." It doesn't check if the thought is fair; it checks if the thought might keep you safe. So it sends more alarms, even when the danger is small or imagined.

Three fast facts (plain language):

- **Repetition builds routes.** The more you think a thought, the faster your brain serves it.
- **Alarms grab attention.** Scary thoughts feel louder because alarms are designed to be loud.
- **Body feedback matters.** If your body feels tense, your brain looks for a reason and often grabs the scariest story nearby.

Good news: new thoughts can also become the default **with practice**.

Common Thought Traps (With Simple Examples)

Thought traps are patterns that keep worry stuck. Spotting them gives you a handle.

- **Catastrophizing**
  Jumping to the worst case.
  "If I make one mistake, I'll ruin everything."

- **Mind Reading**
  Guessing what others think.
  "She didn't text back—she must be mad."

- **All-or-Nothing Thinking**
  Only seeing perfect or terrible.
  "If it's not perfect, it's a failure."

- **Overgeneralizing**
  One bad moment becomes "always."
  "That date went badly; I'll never have a good one."

- **Fortune Telling**
  Predicting the future without facts.
  "I just know this will go wrong."

- **Emotional Reasoning**
  Feeling = fact.
  "I feel scared, so this must be dangerous."

- **Shoulds**
  Rules that tighten shame.
  "I should be over this by now."

- **Labeling**
  Turning a behavior into an identity.
  "I fumbled my words—I'm stupid."

- **Personalizing**
  Taking blame for things outside your control.
  "They were quiet; I must have done something."

- **Intolerance of Uncertainty**
  Needing guarantees to feel safe.
  "If I can't be sure, I can't decide."

You don't need to memorize these. Start by spotting the top **two** types that show up for you.

Why Reframing Works

Reframing means looking at the same moment from a kinder, more accurate angle. You aren't denying feelings. You are cleaning the lens.

- It lowers the alarm. Kinder thoughts reduce body tension.
- It opens choices. When you see more than the worst case, you act differently.
- It trains new routes. Repeated balanced thoughts become easier to find.

Example

Anxious: "I'm going to bomb this presentation."

Reframed: "I'm nervous because I care, and I prepared what I can."

The facts didn't change. The **story** did and that changes your body and your next move.

The Look Step in CALM

This is where you pause and ask:

- "Is there another way to see this?"
- "What would a kinder version sound like?"
- "If I wasn't anxious, how would I describe this?"
- "What facts do I have? What am I guessing?"

You're not chasing perfect thoughts. You're aiming for **truer and kinder**.

The Four-Step Reframe

1. Notice it

- Catch the thought. That's a win.

2. **Name the trap**

- Catastrophizing? Mind reading? All-or-nothing?

3. **Question it**

- "Is this 100% true?"
- "What evidence supports it? What evidence doesn't?"
- "Would I say this to a friend?"
- "What are three other outcomes besides the worst one?"

4. **Soften it**

- Write a balanced line that's **10% kinder** and **closer to the facts**.

Small shift, big change over time.

The Thought Flip Exercise (Guided)

Draw two columns or open a notes app.

Anxious Thought	Balanced Thought
"I'll embarrass myself at the meeting."	"I may feel nervous, and I can still share one clear idea."
"If I say no, they'll be upset."	"People can be disappointed and still respect me."
"One symptom means something is wrong."	"Symptoms can have many causes. I'll note it and check as needed."
"They didn't smile, I did something wrong."	"I don't know their day. I'll ask if needed instead of guessing."

Practice plan: Do three flips a day for one week. Short lines count.

"Worry to Plan" Filter

Ask two questions:

1. **Is this in my control today?**
- Yes → make a **10-minute plan**.
2. No → place it on a "later" list (review at a set time).**What is one next step?**
3. Not ten steps. *One.*

This moves you from spinning to action.

Probability & Impact Box

Write your fear. Then rate:

- **How likely is this?** (0-10)
- **How big is the impact if it happens?** (0-10)
- **What could reduce the impact by 1-2 points?** (small supports, backup plan)

This turns a foggy fear into a clear picture you can work with.

Scale the Fear

- Rate fear now (0-10).
- List three outcomes: worst, best, **most likely**.
- Write one sentence for the most likely.
- Re-rate the fear.

You'll often see the number drop a few points. That shift matters.

Time Travel Test

- **Future you**: "If this happens, how would I cope for the first 24 hours?"
- **Past you**: "When have I handled something hard before? What did I use then?"

Your history counts as evidence.

Thought Parking Lot

Some thoughts need attention; some need **a parking spot**.

- Set a **worry window** (for example, 6:30-6:45 pm).
- When a worry pops up at noon, write it down and tell yourself, "Not now. 6:30."
- At 6:30, review the list for **15 minutes**. Convert any item you can control into one small action. Let the rest wait.

You're not ignoring your mind; you're training it to meet at a set time.

If/Then Coping Plans

Write quick plans for frequent worries.

- "**If** I start to spiral before a meeting, **then** I will do 3 rounds of 4-2-6 breathing and read my top three points."
- "**If** I wake at 2 a.m., **then** I will write one reminder for morning and play my sleep track."
- "**If** I want to cancel a plan because of fear, **then** I will go for 15 minutes and reassess."

Plans reduce guesswork under stress.

Three Helpful Voices (Chair Method)

Picture three chairs in your mind. Move your thoughts through each one.

1. **Scientist** (facts): "What do I know for sure?"
2. **Coach** (kind and firm): "What helps me do the next right thing?"
3. **Friend** (compassion): "What would I say to someone I love?"

Blend the three into a single balanced line.

Scripts You Can Use

Performance (work or school)

- "Nerves mean I care. I'll lead with one clear point."
- "I can prepare, not perfect."

Social

- "Most people are focused on themselves. I'll aim for one real moment."
- "Awkward is part of being human."

Health

- "A symptom is a clue, not a verdict. I'll note, watch, and follow the plan."

Parenting/Caregiving

- "I won't get it right every time. I can repair and reconnect."

Boundaries

- "Saying no protects my yes."

Write your favorite script on a card or in your phone.

Micro-Practices

- **Two-Sentence Rule**
- "I'm noticing the thought that _____. A kinder view is _____."
- **5-Box Thought Record (lite)**
- Trigger → Feeling (0-10) → Anxious thought → Balanced line → Next tiny action
- **1% Kinder**
- Keep the same thought but change one word to soften it. Repeat until it feels doable.

Roadblocks (and Workarounds)

- **"The thought feels 100% true."**
- Try: "It **feels** 100% true." Then add one fact that leans the other way.
- **"I can't think of a balanced line."**
- Borrow one from the scripts. Or ask, "What would I tell a 10-year-old I care about?"
- **"I keep ruminating."**
- Pair reframing with **body anchors** (long exhale, feet on floor) and set a **worry window**.
- **Trauma or OCD patterns**
- If thoughts are graphic, stuck, or drive strong compulsions, add professional support. Reframing can help, but you may need more structured care. Getting help is a strength move.

7-Day Reframe

- **Day 1-2:** Spot your top two traps. Write one example of each.

- **Day 3-4:** Do the Thought Flip for three thoughts a day. Short lines count.
- **Day 5:** Add the **Worry to Plan** filter to one item.
- **Day 6:** Create two **If/Then** coping plans.
- **Day 7:** Review what helped. Keep your best two tools. Drop the rest.

Small and steady wins.

Reflection Questions

1. What types of anxious thoughts pop up most often?
2. Are there phrases you use that make anxiety worse?
3. What fears sit underneath those thoughts?
4. Do you believe every thought that shows up?
5. How do your thoughts change how your body feels?
6. What would a compassionate version of this thought sound like?
7. What's one new way to see this?
8. What evidence supports or contradicts your fear?
9. Who would you be without this thought in charge?
10. How can you practice balanced thinking more often?

Big Takeaway

Thoughts are powerful, *and* they're not always true.

Reframing doesn't erase real problems. It gives you a fair story and a steadier body so *you* can choose your next step.

When you notice, name, question, and soften, even by 10%, you turn a scary narrator into a helpful guide. That's how you get your mind back.

Next up, we'll talk about **Move Forward**, the last step in CALM - how to take action even when anxiety is riding in the passenger seat.

CHAPTER FOUR

MANAGING TRIGGERS AND STRESSORS

Anxiety rarely arrives without knocking. Most of the time, something opens the door for it, a trigger.

Sometimes, that trigger is easy to spot. Maybe you get a call from an unknown number and your stomach drops. Maybe you hear your boss say, "Can I see you for a minute?" and your chest tightens. Maybe you smell a familiar perfume and feel yourself freeze.

Other times, the trigger slips in quietly. You don't notice the moment it happened - you just realize you're suddenly tense, distracted, or ready to run. You catch yourself mid-reaction and think, *Where did that come from?*

This is the nature of triggers. They're not random. They're your brain's way of saying, *Something about this feels familiar. Last time, it wasn't safe. Pay attention.*

The trouble is, your brain doesn't always check the facts. It reacts to the possibility of danger, even when there isn't any.

That's why understanding your triggers, and learning how to work with them, can change your whole relationship with anxiety. It's not about avoiding everything that sets you off. It's about having a plan so you don't get stuck in the reaction.

What Counts as a Trigger?

A **trigger** is any stimulus, something you see, hear, smell, taste, feel, or remember, that sparks an emotional or physical reaction. Your brain has paired that trigger with a past experience of stress, fear, or harm. The pairing is so strong that the reaction can happen in seconds.

Triggers by sense

Sight:

- Seeing a message from someone who's hurt you in the past.
- Walking into a crowded room after months of avoiding social events.
- Passing a street corner where you once had an accident.

Sound:

- Hearing someone raise their voice.
- A loud bang or unexpected noise.
- A song that played during a breakup or loss.

Smell:

- The scent of a hospital disinfectant.
- A certain perfume that belonged to an ex-partner.
- Fresh-cut grass if you once had an emergency outdoors.

Touch:

- A pat on the back that catches you off guard.
- The texture of a fabric tied to a difficult memory.
- The coldness of metal or glass that reminds you of an event.

Taste:

- A food you ate before bad news.
- A drink you had during a stressful conversation.

Thoughts or Memories:

- Remembering something hard, even briefly, can bring back the same body sensations and emotions you had at the time.

Case Example:

I once worked with a client who didn't understand why she'd feel suddenly anxious every time she walked into a certain coffee shop. After some reflection, she realized she had met her ex there for a breakup conversation. The shop's smell, coffee beans mixed with baked goods, had been stored in her body's memory.

The Stress Bucket Effect

Triggers are only part of the story. If you already have a high level of stress, your system will respond to even small triggers as if they're huge threats.

Think of your **stress like a bucket**:

- Every late night, hard conversation, financial worry, or skipped meal adds drops to your bucket.
- If you never empty the bucket, it stays near the top.
- When something small happens, a traffic jam, a sarcastic comment, the bucket spills over.

That spillover is why you might react more strongly on certain days. Your reaction isn't just about the trigger - it's about how full your bucket already is.

Pro tip: Notice what drains your bucket versus what fills it. Both matter.

Emotional Responses That Surprise You

Being triggered can cause unexpected emotional and behavioral changes:

- **Irritability:** Snapping at someone you love over something minor.
- **Tears:** Crying in a meeting without fully understanding why.
- **Withdrawal:** Shutting down mid-conversation, avoiding eye contact.
- **Freeze:** Feeling "stuck" and unable to make a decision.

These are **not** signs of weakness. They're signs your nervous system reacted before your conscious brain caught up. Once that alarm is pulled, your job is not to shame yourself - it's to find ways to lower the volume.

Step 1 - Comfort: Validating Your Experience

The **Comfort** step in CALM starts with permission. You don't have to justify why you feel what you feel.

Ways to validate yourself:
- "My body is trying to protect me. That's not wrong."
- "This reaction makes sense based on what I've been through."
- "I'm allowed to feel this way and still choose how I respond."

Skipping validation and going straight to *"What's wrong with me?"* adds another layer of distress. Comfort removes the shame so you can move toward calming down.

Step 2 - Anchor: Soothing in Real Time

After validating yourself, your next goal is to bring your body back into the present. This is the **Anchor** step - grounding your body so your mind follows.

Grounding options:
- **Breathing reset:** Inhale for 4 counts, hold for 2, exhale for 6. Repeat at least three times.

- **5-4-3-2-1:** Name 5 things you see, 4 you can touch, 3 you hear, 2 you smell, 1 you taste.
- **Physical grounding:** Press your heels into the floor or grip the arms of your chair. Feel the weight of your body being supported.

Practicing these when you're calm builds "muscle memory" so they're easier to use when you're stressed.

Step 3 - Look: Reframing the Trigger

Once your body calms, you can check your thoughts. This is the **Look** step, asking whether your reaction matches the moment you're in.

Questions to try:

- "Is this reaction about right now or about the past?"
- "What would a kinder version of this thought sound like?"
- "If my best friend felt this way, what would I tell them?"

Example:

- Original thought: "I'm falling apart in front of everyone."
- Reframed thought: "I'm having a strong reaction, and I can still recover in this moment."

Step 4 - Move: Preparing for Next Time

You can't erase every trigger. But you can prepare so they don't control you.

Planning ideas:

- **Identify patterns:** Which times of day, environments, or people spark anxiety?
- **Pack your tools:** Keep a mental and/or written list of grounding exercises.

- **Set boundaries:** Limit exposure to situations that consistently drain you.
- **Schedule recovery:** Plan downtime after high-stress situations.

Trigger Mapping Exercise

Try this in your journal or a notes app:

1. **Identify the trigger:** Write down what set you off.
2. **Notice the body reaction:** Where did you feel it? What happened physically?
3. **Label the emotion:** Name the main feeling—fear, anger, sadness, overwhelm.
4. **Check the thought:** What was running through your mind?
5. **Ground yourself:** Write which Comfort or Anchor tool you used.
6. **Reframe:** Write a more balanced way to see it.
7. **Plan:** How will you respond if this happens again?

Doing this over time will reveal patterns and show you how much you're actually improving.

Case Examples - Triggers in Different Settings

Workplace:

- Trigger: Being called on unexpectedly in a meeting.
- Response: Heart races, mind goes blank.
- CALM use: Comfort ("It's okay to feel nervous"), Anchor (slow breathing under the table), Look (reframe: "I can answer one part of the question"), Move (prepare talking points before meetings).

Relationships:

- Trigger: Partner using a certain tone during conflict.
- Response: Immediate defensiveness, urge to leave the room.

- CALM use: Comfort ("I'm reacting to tone, not the content"), Anchor (press feet into the floor), Look (consider if the intent matches my assumption), Move (ask for a pause before responding).

Public Spaces:

- Trigger: Crowded train platform.
- Response: Sweaty palms, rapid breathing.
- CALM use: Comfort ("Crowds feel unsafe to me, and that's okay"), Anchor (focus on 5 things I see), Look (remind myself I've handled this before), Move (stand near an exit for a quicker way out).

10 Reflection Questions

1. What triggered your anxiety most recently?
2. Are there recurring stressors in your environment?
3. How do you usually cope when you're triggered?
4. Do you feel ashamed of your reactions?
5. What helps you feel grounded after being triggered?
6. Can you name what you needed in that moment?
7. Is there a kinder way to see your reaction?
8. What patterns do you notice in your stress response?
9. What's one thing you could do differently next time?
10. How can you build in recovery time after stress hits?

Big takeaway:

Triggers are not proof there's something wrong with you. They're signals from your body saying, *Pay attention, there's something here for you to to care for.*

Every time you meet a trigger with CALM, you're teaching yourself you can handle more than you thought you could. Over time, you'll notice you bounce back a little faster, and anxiety won't feel like it has such a tight hold over your life.

CHAPTER FIVE

THE POWER OF ROUTINE AND HABITS

An anxious brain loves predictability. Not because you're boring, or inflexible, or "can't handle change," but because routines are predictable and predictability feels safe. It's like a warm blanket for your nervous system - a signal saying, *We know what's coming next, no need to be on alert.*

Think about it: If you're walking into a new environment, you're scanning for signs, checking for exits, and trying to figure out where you are supposed to be going. That's mental work. But if you're walking into your favorite restaurant, you know the menu, you know the staff, and you know where the bathrooms are located. Routines work the same way. They take away the constant guessing game and give your mind a break.

Why Predictability Works for an Anxious Mind

Anxiety thrives on uncertainty. The more unknowns your brain has to navigate, the more space it has to fill in the blanks and an anxious brain usually fills those blanks with *worst-case scenarios.*

Here's what routines actually do inside your brain:

1. **They quiet the threat scanner.**
   - Your amygdala (the part of your brain that's always on guard for danger) is less likely to sound the alarm when it recognizes a safe, familiar pattern.
2. **They reduce decision fatigue.**
   - Every choice - what to eat, what to wear, when to call someone back - takes mental energy. When you're anxious, you're already

running a "high-burn" brain. Routines turn some choices into autopilot, saving energy for what matters most.

3. **They give you safety cues.**
- When you repeat certain actions in a predictable way, your brain starts associating them with safety. Over time, these actions can calm you just by starting them, like your morning coffee ritual or evening shower.

4. **They create "anchors" in time.**
- Anchors are consistent points in your day that help you orient yourself emotionally. They tell your brain, *This is where we are in the day, and this is what we do here.*

What a Routine *Isn't*

Before we go further, let's clear up a myth:

A routine is **not** a rigid, minute-by-minute schedule leaving no room for life to happen. That kind of rigidity can make anxiety worse.

Instead, think of routines as **patterns you return to**, steady guideposts that help you stay grounded even when the day goes sideways.

The Three Layers of Routines

To make them work for anxiety, I like to think of routines in **three layers**:

- **Opening Routines** - how you start your day.
- **Maintenance Routines** - what keeps you steady in the middle.
- **Closing Routines**- how you end your day and signal it's safe to rest.

Let's go through each layer in detail.

Opening Routines - Setting the Tone for the Day

How you start your morning matters because your nervous system takes cues from those first waking moments.

If you start in chaos (oversleeping, rushing, checking stressful emails immediately), your brain learns: *We're already behind. Stay on high alert.*

If you start with intention, your brain learns: *We're safe. We can move at a steady pace.*

Ideas for an anxiety-friendly morning:

- Drink a glass of water before you check your phone.
- Do gentle stretches or a short walk to wake up your body.
- Make your bed - not to impress anyone, but to mark that the day has begun.
- Write your top three priorities so your brain isn't juggling a giant mental list.

Case study: A client of mine used to wake up, grab her phone, and immediately dive into work emails. Her mornings were filled with stress before she'd even brushed her teeth. We swapped that habit for five minutes of breathing before touching her phone. Her morning anxiety dropped significantly.

Maintenance Routines - Steadying the Middle of the Day

The middle of the day is where anxiety often sneaks in. Energy starts to dip, stressors pile up, and decision fatigue sets in. This is where **mini-routines** shine.

Anchor examples (keep you grounded in the moment):

- Three slow breaths before starting a meeting.

- Placing your hand on your heart to remind yourself, *I'm here. I'm okay.*
- Drinking water slowly and intentionally.

Move examples (help you take small steps forward):

- Five minutes of desk organization before lunch.
- A quick walk after a tense phone call.
- Sending one "avoidance" email you've been putting off.

Even one or two of these sprinkled throughout your day can keep your anxiety from building to a breaking point.

Closing Routines - Signaling It's Safe to Rest

Your body won't fully relax until it *knows* the day is done. Closing routines create that signal.

Evening wind-down ideas:

- Turn off electronics 30-60 minutes before bed.
- Turn on an essential oil diffuser.
- Journal about your day or read a favorite book.
- Do some gentle stretching.

Tip: Start with small baby steps. A one-minute routine is better than no routine.

Habit Stacking - The Easy Way to Add Good Habits

Habit stacking means pairing a new habit with one you already do all the time - aka the anchor habit.

Examples:

- After brushing your teeth → do a minute of deep breathing.

- After pouring your coffee → write one sentence in a gratitude journal.
- After logging off work → stretch for two minutes.

The "anchor" habit acts like a reminder to do the new one.

Habit Unlearning - Breaking Cycles That Feed Anxiety

Some habits make anxiety worse you don't even realize it.

Examples:

- Using your phone before you get out of bed.
- Staying up late to scroll on social media.
- Saying "yes" to every request even when you're tired.

The key is to replace the negative habit. If you stop doing something but don't fill the gap, your brain will default to the old behavior.

When Routines Break

Life happens. You get sick. You travel. Someone needs you unexpectedly. The anxious brain loves to turn this into a story about failure.

Self-compassion reminders for disrupted routines:

- "This week has been rough. I'll start with one small habit."
- "One off day doesn't erase months of progress."
- "I can always begin again."

Barriers to Routine-Building

1. **Perfectionism:** Waiting until you get it "right" means you never actually start doing it. *Solution:* Begin with the babiest step possible.

2. **All-or-nothing thinking:** Missing one day doesn't mean you suddenly need to quit. *Solution:* Focus on the next opportunity available, instead of the missed opportunity.

3. **Boredom:** Some people feel restless without a lot of change in their lives. *Solution:* Keep the *structure* the same but switch up the *details (i.e. keep the same schedule but change what is done at certain times).*

Practical Routine-Building Exercise

Step 1: Choose one anchor routine (calms your body) and one move routine (gets you moving forward).

Step 2: Attach each to something you already do every day.

Step 3: Practice for one week before adding more.

Example:

- Anchor: Three deep breaths → right before turning on your laptop.
- Move: Send one important email → right after lunch.

Interactive Worksheet: Build Your Anxiety-Friendly Routine

Morning:

- Anchor: _____
- Move: _____

Midday:

- Anchor: _____
- Move: _____

Evening:

- Anchor: _____

- Move: _____

Reflection Questions

1. Which parts of your day feel most chaotic?
2. What's one small ritual that makes you feel safe?
3. How do you react when your routine is disrupted?
4. What's one morning habit you could start tomorrow?
5. What's one evening habit you could add this week?
6. Which habits might be increasing your anxiety?
7. When do you feel most grounded in your day?
8. Which old habit could you replace with something healthier?
9. How would your anxiety change if your day had more predictability?
10. How can you restart gently after falling off track?

Big Takeaway:

Routines aren't about perfection. Not at all. They're about giving your brain a break, helping you feel safe, and making it easier to bounce back after stress.

When anxiety says, *We don't know what's next.* Your routines answer: *yes we do and we're good*

CHAPTER SIX

ANXIETY IN A COMPLICATED WORLD

Anxiety doesn't only come from inside you. It often comes from the world you live in.

Headlines. Sirens. Loud arguments online. New rules. Big changes. Scary losses.

When the world feels shaky, your body feels it. Your mind scans for danger. Your heart works harder. Your sleep gets light. Your thoughts speed up.

You're not "too sensitive." You're human. And you can learn to steady yourself, even when the world is loud.

This chapter gives you a steady way to face **global and social stress** using **CALM**:

- **Comfort** - name the pain without shame
- **Anchor** - settle your body in the here and now
- **Look** - see the story with kinder, clearer eyes
- **Move** - take one small step that fits your values

You'll get tools, short scripts, and simple plans you can use right away. Keep what helps. Leave the rest.

How Big-World Stress Hits Your Body (Plain Talk)

Your brain has an alarm system. When you sense a threat, the alarm turns on. Your body moves into **fight, flight, freeze, or fawn**. This can happen even when the threat is far away. That's called **secondary** or **vicarious** stress. You care, so your body reacts.

Common signs:

- Tight chest or shallow breath
- Jaw clenching, headaches
- Doomscrolling you can't stop
- Numbness, snapping at people, or feeling "checked out"
- Light sleep, tense dreams, early waking

You're not broken. Your alarm is loud. We can turn it down.

90 Second Mini reset:

1. Exhale long.
2. Inhale 4, hold 2, exhale 6 (repeat 5 times).
3. Name 3 things you can see, 2 you can touch, 1 sound you hear.
4. Drop your shoulders. Unclench your jaw. Uncurl your toes.

The Control Triangle

Draw a triangle with three layers:

- **Top - Control:** your breath, your voice, your choices, your vote, your giving, your routine
- **Middle - Influence:** your home, friends, team, school, local groups
- **Bottom - Concern:** world events you care about but can't change alone

Spend most energy at the **top** and **middle**. Visit the **bottom** in **short, planned windows**.

Check-in question:

Where did I spend energy today - Control, Influence, or Concern?

CALM for Big Topics (Deep Dive + Doable Steps)

Each section gives: how it may feel, **CALM** steps, a short case story, and scripts you can use.

1) War and Humanitarian Crises

Feels like: fear for loved ones, guilt for being safe, anger, grief, nonstop checking.

Comfort

- "It makes sense that I'm scared and sad."
- "Caring hurts because I care deeply."

Anchor

- Hold a hope object (stone, bracelet, faith item).
- 4–2–6 breaths before and after news.
- Hand on heart + finger on map: "There is there. Here is me."

Look

- "I can't fix everything. I can choose one kind act."
- "Helpers are working each day."

Move

- Donate what you can (even $5).
- Write one letter, light one candle, attend one vigil.
- News windows: 10–15 minutes, 1–2 times/day. Then step away.

Case – Nadia

Her cousin is in a conflict zone. Morning and evening check-ins only. Small monthly gift. News windows. Her anxiety drops from 9 to 6. She sleeps.

Script (to a friend):

"I'm limiting crisis news to two windows a day so I can stay present. If there's urgent family news, please text me."

2) Immigration Uncertainty and Displacement

Feels like: fear of papers, deadlines, travel holds, separation, and language stress.

Comfort

- "Of course I'm on edge. Safety matters."
- "Asking for help is wise."

Anchor

- "Folder ritual": sit, drink water, breathe, then open documents.
- Keep a **hope kit** (IDs, contacts, meds list) in one safe place.

Look

- "Next step, not the whole mountain."
- "I can learn with support."

Move

- Contact list: lawyer, clinic, school, community org.
- Two weekly "paper hours" with a buddy/interpreter.
- Practice key phrases in your language and the local one.

Script (office):

"Hello, English is not my first language. Can someone explain my case in simple steps or another language?"

Case - Luis

He sets "paper hours" Sundays 2-3 pm. He keeps a document checklist. Each week one box gets a check. Fear drops from 8 to 5.

3) Political Instability and Election Stress

Feels like: anger, dread, family fights, tight chest, late-night scrolling.

Comfort

- "This is tense. It affects my life."
- "I can care and rest."

Anchor

- During election week: walk before screens; breathe while coffee brews; Do Not Disturb after 9 p.m.

Look

- "My power lives in my plan: register, research, vote."
- "Online fights rarely change hearts. Relationships do."

Move

- Ballot plan (where, when, ID).
- One short volunteer shift or offer rides to the polls.
- Keep news to windows, not all day.

Script (family):

"I love you. I'm getting flooded. Can we pause and continue tomorrow?"

Case - Priya

She made a vote plan, muted political threads at night, and joined a two-hour phone bank. She felt less helpless, more focused.

4) Economic Turmoil and Inflation

Feels like: math fear, bill dread, shame, "I'll never catch up."

Comfort

- "Money stress is about safety. Of course I feel it."

- "This is hard and does not define my worth."

Anchor

- Money ritual: feet flat, 5 slow breaths, open one bill.
- Two weekly "money windows" (calendar it).

Look

- "Information helps me steer."
- "Small steps count: $5 to savings, one call for a plan."

Move

- Cancel one unused subscription.
- Ask to move a due date to paycheck day.
- Start a tiny "calm fund."

Script (company):

"I'm reviewing my bill. Are there payment plans or hardship options?"

Case - Danika

Ten-minute money date on Tuesdays. Canceled two subs. Asked for a due-date shift. Late fees stopped. Sleep improved.

For more tools, see the Financial Anxiety Chapter.

5) Climate Change and Environmental Fear

Feels like: grief for places, storm fear, guilt, anger, pressure to do everything.

Comfort

- "This hurts because I love this Earth."
- "I can hold grief and still act."

Anchor

- Get outside daily if you can: tree, sky, sun, breeze.
- Hold a leaf or stone. Breathe with it.

Look

- "Circle of control + community."
- "Many are working on solutions."

Move

- "One square meter of care": water, weed, pick up litter.
- Lower energy use one small way.
- Join one local project a month.

Case - Mateo

He started "Ten-Minute Yard Care" each evening. He joined a neighborhood tree-plant day. Mood lifted. Doomscrolling dropped.

6) Public Safety, Mass Violence, Civil Unrest

Feels like: jumpy in crowds, fear at events, hyper-vigilance, nightmares.

Comfort

- "My alarm is trying to protect me."
- "Prepared, not panicked."

Anchor

- Before public spaces: three slow breaths; spot exits and helpers; set a buddy text.
- After events: shake arms and legs, slow walk, warm shower.

Look

- "I'm allowed to leave early."

- "I can plan safety without living in fear."

Move

- Family safety plan (meeting point, contacts).
- Save emergency numbers in favorites.
- Take a basic first-aid class with a friend.

Script (to host):

"Where's the quiet space if I need a reset?"

7) Cultural Identity Stress and Discrimination

Feels like: being watched, questioned, erased; microaggressions; body on alert.

Comfort

- "My dignity is not up for debate."
- "It makes sense that my body stays ready."

Anchor

- Hand on heart or grounding item tied to identity (scarf, bracelet, faith token).
- Pride line: "I belong. I am enough."

Look

- "That behavior was harmful. I'm allowed to respond or not."
- "I'll choose the time and place that is safest for me."

Move

- Script: "I don't use that term. Here's why…" or "That comment is harmful. Please don't say it to me again."
- Log incidents; seek support (HR, ombud, union, trusted leader).
- Spend time in spaces where your identity is honored.

Case - Asha

A coworker joked about her hair. She used: "Please don't comment on my body or hair." She logged it, met with HR, found an affinity group. Her body settled.

8) Media Overexposure and Compassion Fatigue

Feels like: numb one day, flooded the next; guilt when you turn it off; can't stop scrolling.

Comfort

- "Breaks protect my care. Rest helps me keep showing up."
- "I'm one person. I matter."

Anchor

- **News windows** only (10–15 minutes, 1–2 times/day).
- After each: stand, breathe, drink water, look outside.

Look

- "Depth over endless bites."
- "I'll follow a few trusted sources."

Move

- Unfollow accounts that spike dread or shame.
- Add two that teach or soothe.
- Replace one scroll with a body break (walk, stretch, one song dance).

Case - Theo

He set news windows at 8 a.m. and 6 p.m. He muted "breaking" alerts. His mood smoothed out. Focus at work grew.

9) Health Crises and Public Health Mistrust

Feels like: fear of illness, worry about access, confusion about changing guidance, mistrust from past harm.

Comfort

- "My health worries make sense."
- "It's okay to ask questions until I understand."

Anchor

- Before appointments/news: 4-2-6 breaths; write three questions.
- Bring a support person on speaker or in person.

Look

- "Please use plain language."
- "Second opinions are allowed."
- "What do we know today? What are my top two choices?"

Move

- Care file: meds, allergies, providers, insurance card, emergency contact.
- Call clinics about low-cost options.
- Schedule brief but regular check-ins.

Script (with a provider):

"I want to understand. Can you explain in steps and share the pros and cons of the top two options?"

Case - Mr. Lee

He feared clinics after a bad past event. He brought his daughter, used his question list, and asked for plain language. He felt seen and followed his care plan.

For more information see the Health Anxiety Chapter.

10) Misinformation and Social Division

Feels like: confusion, fear, anger, fights with friends or family, "Who do I trust?"

Comfort

- "Feeling confused means the info is messy, not that I'm failing."
- "I can slow down before I share."

Anchor

- When a shocking post pops up: put the phone down, 3 slow breaths, drink water.

Look

- Three checks: **Who said it? What's the source? Can I verify elsewhere?**
- "If it's urgent and scary, I'll confirm before I pass it on."

Move

- Save a short list of trusted sources.
- Avoid public comment fights. Choose private, caring talks.
- Take a 24-hour pause before replying if you're hot.

Script (with loved one):

"I care about you. I'm seeing different info. Can we swap sources and talk when we're both calm?"

Case - Hana

She paused before sharing posts. She checked two sources first. Her family chats got calmer. Fewer fights. More care.

A Daily CALM Plan for a Complicated World

Morning (3-4 min)

- Comfort: "Today may be loud. I can be kind to me."
- Anchor: 3 breaths before screens.
- Look: "What matters most in my circle today?"
- Move: choose one tiny step.

Midday (2-3 min)

- Stand, shoulders down, sip water.
- If needed, a 10-minute news window. Then step away.

Evening (5-8 min)

- Short walk or stretch.
- Write one win and one care you gave yourself.
- Tech off 30–60 minutes before bed.

A Weekly CALM Reset

- What shook me this week? What helped?
- Which tool worked fastest - Comfort, Anchor, Look, or Move?
- What boundary will I try next week? (fewer alerts, one news window, one no-screen evening)
- What small action will I take for a cause I care about? (email, donation, meeting, check on a neighbor)

Siren Plan for Breaking News

When a big alert hits:

1. **Comfort:** "It's normal to feel this."
2. **Anchor:** 5 slow breaths, feet on floor, drink water.
3. **Look:** Find one trusted source; skip comment threads.

4. **Move:** Brief action if you can (share a resource, check a loved one). Then step away.
5. **Close:** two minutes outside or by a window; soft music; short stretch.

Children and Teens: How to Talk About Hard News

- Start with questions: "What have you heard? How are you feeling?"
- Keep it simple: "Some people were hurt. Helpers are there now."
- Share your plan and local helpers.
- Anchor together: draw, breathe, take a walk, keep bedtime steady.
- Limit replays of scary footage.

Kid script:

"You can ask me anything. If I don't know, we'll find out together."

For more information see the Anxiety Across Life Stages Chapter.

For Helpers, Healers, and Advocates

If you teach, treat, organize, or care for others, you carry extra weight.

- **Dose your exposure:** set limits before long days.
- **Pair hard with soft:** after tough work, add rest, food, movement, laughter.
- **Debrief:** 10 minutes with a peer, not just a screen.
- **Rotate** roles if you can: info-finding, calling, logistics, rest.
- **Watch red flags:** no sleep, no appetite, numbness, rage spikes, dread of work—reach out for support.

For more information see the Caregiver Anxiety Chapter

Boundaries Lab (Practice and Scripts)

News windows

- "I'm staying informed at 8 a.m. and 6 p.m. only."

Social ask

- "I'm off heavy content this week. If something directly affects me, please text."

Family limit

- "I want relationship first. Let's switch topics and come back later."

Workplace

- "I'm impacted by recent events. May I take a 10-minute reset and return focused?"

Community

- "I can give two hours this month. Where is that most useful?"

Worksheets (Print or Copy)

A) Control Triangle

Control (top): _____

Influence (middle): _____

Concern (bottom): _____

Circle where you spent energy today. Star where you want to spend more tomorrow.

B) News Window Plan

Source(s): _____

Times: _____

Closing ritual (stretch, tea, window): _____

C) Action Ladder

Step 1 (2 min): _____

Step 2 (10 min): _____

Step 3 (monthly): _____

D) Identity Care Map

Safe people: _____

Safe places: _____

Safe words/lines: _____

Rest practices: _____

E) Body Signal Tracker (7 days)

Signs I felt (jaw, chest, sleep): _____

What helped (C/A/L/M): _____

How long to settle: _____

Reflection Questions

1. What recent world events left you unsettled?
2. What emotions show up when you read or watch the news?

3. How much media helps you stay aware? When does it tip into overwhelm?

4. What helps you feel rooted when the world feels shaky?

5. Which communities or causes feel like "home" to you?

6. How do you tend to react—numb, panic, hyper-aware?

7. What are three things you can control today?

8. What boundary with the news would serve you this week?

9. What small act of care could you offer yourself or someone else today?

10. How can you hold both awareness and peace at the same time?

11. What value do you want to center this month (kindness, truth, service, rest)?

12. What is one conversation you can have that builds connection, not division?

13. Where could you swap online time for local action?

14. What helps you close the day even when the world is heavy?

15. Who is your "check-in" person when sirens are loud?

Takeaway

The world can be heavy. Your anxiety makes sense. You don't have to carry everything alone. With **CALM**, you can respond with presence, not panic:

- **Comfort** says your feelings are valid.
- **Anchor** brings your body back now.
- **Look** widens the view.
- **Move** turns care into action.

One breath. One boundary. One baby step.

Repeat as needed.

CHAPTER SEVEN

SOCIAL ANXIETY

Social anxiety can feel like walking into a room and suddenly being handed a microphone you never asked for. In that moment, your awareness becomes laser-focused on everything: the sound of your voice, whether your shirt is sitting strangely, the way people might be looking at you. This hypervigilance doesn't require a major event like giving a presentation or delivering a speech—it can be triggered by something as routine as ordering food, hitting "send" on a text message, or navigating the checkout line at the grocery store.

When social anxiety takes hold, your mind often spirals into "what if" scenarios that feel both urgent and overwhelming:

- *What if they think I'm weird?*
- *What if I say the wrong thing?*
- *What if they can tell I'm nervous?*

Reframing Your Experience

If these thoughts feel familiar, it's important to understand what's really happening. This experience doesn't mean you're inherently socially awkward or destined to struggle with relationships forever. Instead, it means your brain is working overtime in its attempts to protect you. Social anxiety represents your nervous system's alarm bells ringing, signaling: "I'm on high alert because this situation feels dangerous."

The challenge lies in recognizing that your brain has miscalibrated its threat detection system. It's treating ordinary human interactions—the very connections that can bring joy, support, and meaning to your life—

as if they were life-or-death situations requiring immediate defensive action.

A Path Forward

Here's the encouraging truth: you don't have to remain trapped in this cycle. Rather than fighting against your brain's protective instincts, you can learn to work with them. With the right tools and understanding, you can gradually transform social situations from feeling like a battlefield into experiences you navigate with increasing confidence and genuine ease.

The journey from social anxiety to social confidence isn't about eliminating all nervousness—it's about changing your relationship with those feelings and developing skills that help you engage authentically with others despite the discomfort.

Why Social Anxiety Exists

Social anxiety is rooted in one of our oldest survival instincts: the need to belong. Thousands of years ago, your life depended on being part of a group. This group protected one another from danger, shared resources, and raised children together. Being rejected by the group? That could mean being left alone to survive in the wild without any support or resources.

Fast-forward to today: you're not surviving in the wild and fending off wild animals, but your brain doesn't know that. It still treats rejection like a threat to your survival. So, when you imagine being judged, embarrassed, or left out your nervous system reacts as if your safety is at stake.

This is why something like introducing yourself can trigger the same fight-or-flight reaction as running from a predator. Your brain's logic is, *If they don't like me, I might not belong. If I don't belong, I'm in danger.*

How Social Anxiety Shows Up

Social anxiety isn't always loud and obvious. Sometimes it's physical: your heart races, your palms sweat, your face gets hot. Other times it's more like a quiet background hum:

- Worrying about saying the "wrong" thing.
- Rehearsing what you'll say before you say it.
- Avoiding events entirely because the thought of going drains you.
- Skipping small moments of connection, like eye contact or waving, because it feels too vulnerable.

I once had a client who hated Zoom calls. She was convinced everyone could see her hands shaking. The truth? Most people were too busy worrying about whether *they* looked awkward on camera. That's one of the ironies of social anxiety, while you're focused on yourself, everyone else is usually focused on themselves too.

The Core Fears Behind Social Anxiety

Most social anxiety boils down to three fears:

1. **The Fear of Judgment** - You imagine others are analyzing your every move.
2. **The Fear of Rejection** - You're afraid you won't be accepted or liked.
3. **The Fear of Awkwardness** - You dread moments where you don't know what to say or do.

And here's the thing: even when the fear isn't realistic, your body reacts as if it's happening. That's why your hands might shake *before* you've even spoken. Your brain has already played out a whole scene of embarrassment, and your nervous system is along for the ride.

The CALM Approach to Social Anxiety

We're going to walk through how each step of my **CALM Framework** can be applied to social anxiety.

Step 1 - Comfort: Creating Internal Safety

You can't control every social situation. You can't control people's thoughts, their reactions, or whether they "get" you. But you can control how safe you feel inside your own skin.

Ways to create comfort before and during social situations:

- **Affirm your right to be there**: Whisper to yourself, "I'm allowed to take up space here."
- **Dress for confidence**: Wear something that's comfortable and makes you feel good, not something you'll be tugging at all night.
- **Plan an exit option**: Give yourself permission to take a short break, step outside, or find a quiet corner if you start to feel overwhelmed.

Comfort is not about avoiding - it's about having a lifeline so you can stay engaged without feeling trapped.

Step 2 - Anchor: Grounding Before and During Social Events

Think of pre-event rituals as warm-ups for your nervous system. They send your brain the message: *We're ready. We're safe.*

Pre-event grounding rituals:

- **Breathing reset**: Inhale for 4, hold for 2, exhale for 6. Repeat three times before entering.
- **Visualization**: Picture yourself walking in with calm body language, smiling, and making small connections.

- **Comfort object**: Keep a small, touchable item—a ring, a bracelet, a smooth stone—that you can reach for when you need a reminder to stay present.

Step 3 - Look: Reframing Social Fears

Your anxious brain is giving you one version of the story—but there are always other angles.

Example reframes:

- Fear: "Everyone will notice I'm awkward."
- Reframe: "Most people are too busy thinking about themselves to notice."
- Fear: "If I stumble over my words, I've ruined everything."
- Reframe: "One awkward moment doesn't define the whole conversation."
- Fear: "If they don't like me, I've failed."
- Reframe: "Not every connection has to be deep, sometimes showing up is enough."

Reframing isn't lying to yourself, it's expanding the lens so you're not stuck in the worst-case view.

Step 4 - Move: Post-Event Reset

After a social event, your brain will want to run the "post-game replay," listing every possible misstep. Instead of letting that spiral, guide it toward reflection and growth.

Post-event reset steps:

1. **Find the wins**: "I showed up. I spoke to at least one person."
2. **Note progress**: Compare it to a past attempt, maybe you stayed longer this time or spoke to more people.

3. **Set a small next goal**: Something simple, like greeting one new person at the next event.

The 4-Week Social Confidence Practice Plan

We're not aiming for "never anxious again." We're aiming for "anxiety doesn't run the show." This 4-week plan builds your confidence step by step.

Week 1 - Small, Safe Wins

- Choose one low-stakes interaction each day (greeting the cashier, making eye contact with a neighbor).
- End each day by writing down one thing you did that showed courage.

Week 2 - Controlled Challenges

- Add slightly more challenging situations (starting a conversation at work, making a phone call you've been avoiding).
- Use your Comfort and Anchor tools before and during.

Week 3 - Group Practice

- Attend one group event, even if small (book club, class, networking coffee).
- Focus on connecting with just one or two people, not "working the room."

Week 4 - Stretch and Reflect

- Try something outside your comfort zone (sharing an opinion in a meeting, introducing yourself to someone new).
- Reflect on the month: What felt easier? What still feels hard? Where did you surprise yourself?

10 Reflection Questions for Social Growth

1. What social situations increase your anxiety?
2. What do you assume others are thinking about you?
3. Do you replay social moments after they happen?
4. How do you comfort yourself during discomfort?
5. What does safety look like in your relationships?
6. What are you most afraid people will notice?
7. Is there a different way to interpret your anxiety?
8. How do you show up when you're not anxious?
9. What would success in a social situation look like to you?
10. How can you practice confidence in small ways?

Your New Story About Social Anxiety

Social anxiety isn't a flaw, it's an overprotective alarm system. By creating ways to feel comfort, grounding yourself before and during events, reframing your fears, and take baby steps, you can train your brain to see social connection as safe instead of dangerous.

Over time, this won't just help you manage social situations, it helps you enjoy them. Or, at the very least, walk away knowing you showed up for yourself in a way you can be proud of.

CHAPTER EIGHT

WORKPLACE ANXIETY

Work can feel like a stage you never asked to be on. The lights are bright, the audience is silent, and every move you make feels like it's being given a grade. For some people, a big presentation can bring on the nerves. For others, it's opening their email first thing in the morning and seeing that their boss has "just a few notes." And for many, it's not just one big moment, but instead it's the steady pressure sitting on your shoulders from dawn til dusk.

Workplace anxiety is not just "being stressed about work." It's a mix of pressure, perfectionism, fear of judgment, and self-doubt that can follow you into every task, meeting, and decision. And if you're not careful, it comes home with you.

The good news is, there are real, practical ways to understand it, manage it, and keep it from running the show.

Why Work Activates Anxiety

There are reasons your brain gets louder at work and none of them mean you're weak or incapable.

- **Performance Pressure** - That feeling like every task needs to be your absolute best work. You tell yourself, "I can't mess up," even when you're working under impossible conditions.
- **Perfectionism** - Believing that one mistake will erase all the good work you've ever done. This turns even small assignments into massive mental tests.

- **High Stakes** - Worrying about your job security, your reputation, or how your boss and/or coworkers see you.
- **Constant Comparison** - Watching what others are doing and feeling like you never measure up.

Your brain often treats the workplace like a survival arena (kind of like the Hunger Games). That's why it stays on high alert, trying to protect you from making mistakes or being rejected, but the side effect is constant exhaustion.

How Anxiety Shows Up at Work

Workplace anxiety doesn't look the same for everyone. It might be loud and obvious, or quiet and sneaky.

The loud signs might be:

- A racing heart before a meeting.
- Sweaty palms when giving a presentation.
- Trouble sleeping before a big deadline.

The quieter signs might be:

- Re-reading emails 10 times before hitting send.
- Over-preparing for meetings and still worrying it's not enough.
- Avoiding new opportunities because you're afraid to fail.
- Saying "yes" to everything to prove your worth.
- Working long hours, not because it's required, but because you feel guilty stopping.

The Inner Critic at Work

Workplace anxiety often comes with an internal voice that's way too harsh. This "inner critic" says things like:

- "You're not doing enough."
- "If you don't get this perfect, you'll look bad."
- "They probably regret hiring you."

The truth? That voice is rarely accurate. But because it's so loud and familiar, it can feel like fact.

To start shifting it, ask:

- Do I focus more on what went wrong than what went well?
- Do I downplay my wins? ("It wasn't a big deal" or "Anyone could've done that.")
- Do I give myself credit for my effort, not just the outcome?

Anchors for Meetings, Deadlines, and High-Pressure Moments

When anxiety spikes, you need something that tells your body, "it's safe enough to focus right now." Anchors can help you do that.

Try these:

- Place both hands flat on your thighs and notice the solid support beneath you. What do you pants feel like, the muscles underneath, etc.
- Hold a pen or small object and focus on its weight and texture.
- Take 3-5 slow, deep breaths before answering a question.
- Keep a calming phrase ready, like, *One thing at a time.*

Don't wait until you're overwhelmed to use an anchor, start before the anxiety builds (kind of like preventative medical care for anxiety).

Reframing Workplace "Failure"

In an anxious mind, even a small mistake can feel like the end of your career. But mistakes are a normal part of learning and growth.

Instead of thinking:

- "I blew it. They'll never trust me again."
- **Try:**
- "I learned something I can use next time."
- "This is one moment in a bigger picture."
- "I can fix this without tearing myself apart."

When you reframe, you teach your brain that mistakes aren't a danger, they're part of the process.

Celebrating Small Wins

Progress isn't just about promotions or big accomplishments. It's built on small, consistent actions.

Examples of small wins:

- Speaking up in a meeting when you usually stay quiet.
- Finishing a task you've been avoiding.
- Asking for help instead of silently struggling.

Celebrating these moments keeps you motivated and shows you that growth is possible, even in small steps.

Managing Feedback Without Spiraling

For many, feedback is the fastest path to an anxiety spiral. Your brain hears one piece of criticism and ignores everything else.

Try this approach:

1. **Pause before reacting** - Take a breath and let your body settle.
2. **Find the useful part** - Pull out one thing you can use to improve.**Separate worth from work** - Remember, feedback is about a task, not your value as a person.

Creating a Balanced Workday

Anxiety thrives in chaos. The more rhythm you give your day, the calmer your nervous system will be.

Ideas:

- **Start with grounding** - 5 minutes of breathing, journaling, or stretching before you check email.
- **Set mini-breaks** - Step away for water, movement, or a reset every couple of hours.
- **Protect your stop time** - Decide when work ends, and actually honor it.

The CALM Workplace Plan - 4 Weeks to a Healthier Work Mindset

This plan uses the CALM framework to make small, realistic changes each week.

Week 1 - Comfort

- Identify your top three workplace triggers.
- Add one comfort habit before starting work (e.g., a calming playlist, a 5-minute stretch).

Week 2 - Anchor

- Choose one grounding technique to use before meetings or deadlines.
- Practice it even on low-stress days so it becomes automatic.

Week 3 - Look

- Pick one recurring anxious thought about work.
- Reframe it daily into something balanced and supportive.

Week 4 - Move

- Set one small, achievable workplace goal (e.g., share one idea in a meeting, delegate a task).
- Celebrate it when you follow through.

10 Reflection Questions

1. What about work makes you anxious?
2. Are you afraid of making mistakes?
3. How do you talk to yourself after a stressful day?
4. What helps you feel calm before high-pressure moments?
5. What do you define as "success" in your job?
6. How do you handle feedback or criticism?
7. Can you reframe a mistake as growth?
8. What tiny win at work can you celebrate today?
9. Do you give yourself permission to rest?
10. What does a balanced workday look like to you?

The Big Takeaway

Workplace anxiety doesn't mean you're bad at your job, it means you care. But caring doesn't have to mean carrying constant fear. By using anchors to steady yourself, reframing mistakes, celebrating progress, and protecting your mental space, you can show up and perform without anxiety being in charge.

When your brain says, *"You're not doing enough,"* your calmer self can answer, *"I'm doing what matters and I'm allowed to breathe while I do it."*

CHAPTER NINE

FINANCIAL ANXIETY

Let's talk about money and the kind of anxiety that sits deep in your body. Not the kind a spreadsheet fixes in five minutes. I mean the stomach-drop when you open a bill. The heat in your face when a card declines. The swirl of thoughts before you check your bank app. Money touches survival, safety, identity, and family history. So of course it's emotional.

This chapter isn't a budgeting class. It's a care plan for your **nervous system** around money. We'll use **CALM (Comfort, Anchor, Look, Move)** to help you feel steadier, even if the numbers are still a work in progress.

Why Financial Anxiety Feels So Heavy

Money = safety. Your brain links money to food, housing, medicine, and care for people you love. When money feels tight, your body reads that as danger. Your alarm system turns up: fast heart, tight chest, upset stomach, shaky hands.

Money = story. Maybe you grew up hearing, "We don't talk about money," or "We never have enough." Maybe you had to grow up fast and pay bills early. Maybe you were told having debt makes you "bad." These messages don't disappear. They sit in your nervous system and show up when you face numbers.

Money = comparison. Friends, coworkers, and social media can make it seem like everyone else is "ahead." Comparison adds shame. Shame makes you avoid. Avoidance creates more mess. Now the spiral is running the show.

The shame–avoid cycle

1. A bill arrives →
2. Your body alarms →
3. Shame voice: "You're failing" →
4. Avoid checking →
5. Late fees, more stress →
6. More shame, more avoidance

We're going to interrupt that loop with CALM. Piece by piece. Breath by breath. Step by tiny step.

The CALM Framework for Money

C - Comfort: Name it without shame

Anxiety multiplies in silence. Comfort starts with truth-telling and kindness.

Try these lines

- "This is hard, and it makes sense that I'm stressed."
- "I'm not the only one facing this."
- "I can learn new money skills at any age."

Practice: Top-3 Fears

Write your top 3 money fears. Don't fix them. Just name them. Then add:

"It's okay to feel this. Many people feel this too."

Practice: Money Story Timeline

Draw a simple line for your life. Mark key money moments: first job, first bill, debt, help received, wins, losses. Circle one event that still stings. Place a hand on your chest and say, "Of course that shaped me." This is Comfort-less judgment, more care.

Myths to release

- "If I were responsible, I'd never feel anxious about money."
- "Debt means I'm a failure."
- "I should know everything without help."

Truer statements

- Responsible people have feelings.
- Debt is a tool and a situation, not a moral score.
- Learning is not shameful; it's wise.

A - Anchor: Help your body feel safe while you face numbers

Before any money task, calm the body. We make better choices when the alarm isn't blaring.

Build a 5 minute Money Check-In Ritual

1. Sit where your feet touch the floor.
2. Put one hand on your chest, one on your belly.
3. Breathe in for 4, hold 2, out for 6 (repeat 5 times).
4. Name 3 things you can see, 2 you can touch, 1 you can hear.
5. Open the bill or app. Stay slow.

Create a Sensory Anchor Kit

- Soft item (blanket, scarf)
- Grounding object (stone, coin, bracelet)
- Calming scent (tea, lotion)
- Keep it where you pay bills. Your body learns: "When these items come out, I can settle."

Set "Money Windows"

Pick two times a week for money tasks (e.g., Tuesday 6–6:20 pm and Saturday 10-10:30 am). Outside those windows, you don't poke the bear.

Inside those windows, you show up with your ritual. Regular rhythm lowers fear.

Body cues to watch

- Jaw clench → soften your face and unstick your tongue from the roof of your mouth
- Shoulders up by ears → roll them back and down
- Breath short and fast → lengthen the exhale

Anchoring isn't a reward for when you've handled everything. Anchoring is how you *start*.

L - Look: Reframe the story your mind is telling

Anxiety loves harsh, final thoughts. We're going to soften and balance them.

Common money thought traps

- **Catastrophizing:** "I'll never get out of this."
- **All-or-nothing:** "If I can't pay it all, why pay anything?"
- **Personalizing:** "This is all my fault."
- **Mind-reading:** "They think I'm irresponsible."
- **Fortune-telling:** "This will ruin everything."

Thought Flips (use these as training wheels)

- "I'll never get out of this." → "This will take time and steps—and I can take one today."
- "I'm bad with money." → "I'm learning skills I wasn't taught."
- "If I ask for help, I've failed." → "Information is support, not shame."
- "One mistake proves I can't handle money." → "One mistake is a lesson, not a label."

- "Everyone else is ahead." → "I'm seeing highlights, not full stories."

Values Check

Ask: *What kind of person do I want to be with money today?* Kind, steady, honest, courageous, generous in small ways? Values guide decisions when fear is loud.

Compare-and-Despair 7 Day Detox

Mute five accounts that trigger shame. Follow three that teach or calm. Notice your body after a week.

M - Move: One tiny, doable step

Small steps beat big plans you never start. Pick a step so easy it feels almost silly.

Low-lift win list

- Open the envelope (don't pay yet).
- Check balances with your ritual.
- Cancel one unused subscription.
- Put $5 in a "calm fund."
- Set one bill reminder on your calendar.
- Email to ask for a payment date or plan.
- Make a list of all debts without judgment (info is power).

The P-P-P Pause (Pause-Plan-Proceed)

- **Pause:** 3 slow breaths.
- **Plan:** "What's the next tiny step?"
- **Proceed:** Do just that step. Then stop.

10-Minute Weekly Money Date (weekly)

Timer on. One small task. When the timer ends, you're done. Reward: tea, music, short walk. Keep it gentle so your brain doesn't fear the date.

Case Stories

Tasha-single parent, surprise bill

A dentist bill is bigger than expected.

- **Comfort:** "Anyone would feel stressed. This doesn't define me as a parent."
- **Anchor:** Hand on chest, 4-2-6 breathing, cold water on wrists.
- **Look:** "I have options: call, ask questions, request a plan."
- **Move:** Call to ask about itemized charges and a payment plan. Set first $20.
- Anxiety doesn't vanish, but it drops from a 9 to a 6. That space matters.

Eli-credit card shame

Afraid to open statements.

- **Comfort:** "Avoiding makes sense when I feel judged."
- **Anchor:** Money ritual + favorite playlist.
- **Look:** "Information helps me steer."
- **Move:** Open statements, write totals, pick one call to ask about interest or hardship options.

Sofía & Malik - money fights

One is a spender, one is a saver.

- **Comfort:** "We both want safety."
- **Anchor:** Sit side-by-side, feet grounded, hands holding a smooth stone they pass back and forth.

- **Look:** "We are fighting fear, not each other."
- **Move:** Set a weekly 20-minute "money talk" with two rules: one agenda, no blame. End with a next step and a thank-you.

Mr. Randolph - fixed income

Rising costs, same check.

- **Comfort:** "Worry doesn't mean weakness; it means I care."
- **Anchor:** Tea, slow breathing, light stretch.
- **Look:** "I'll ask the clinic and utility company about senior plans."
- **Move:** Call the pharmacy about generics; ask the power company for budget billing.

Scripts You Can Borrow

Calling a company (payment plan)

"Hi, I'm reviewing my bill and I'm concerned about affording the full amount. Are there payment plan options or a hardship program I can apply for?"

Asking for a due date change

"I'm paid on the 15th. Can we move my due date to match that schedule?"

Talking to a partner

"I feel scared when unexpected costs come up. I'd like a short, weekly check-in with a clear agenda so we can plan together."

With friends (spending boundary)

"I'm saving right now, so I'm skipping the dinner out. I'd love a walk or coffee at home instead."

When someone asks to borrow

"I can't lend money, but I can help you look for options or make some calls."

Short. Clear. Kind.

Boundaries That Protect Your Peace

- Pick **money windows** and stick to them.
- No money talks after a set time at night.
- Use *Do Not Disturb* during your money date.
- Decline events that don't fit your season. Offer a lower-cost plan.
- Share your limits early: "I can give this amount," or "I can't this time."

Boundaries are not rejection. They are care for you and for your future.

Holidays, Gifts, and Social Pressure

- Make a simple list and a simple limit.
- Give time, notes, or help as gifts. Meaning doesn't have to be pricey.
- Plan "no-spend" traditions: game nights, potlucks, photo swaps, service days.
- When someone spends big on you, say thank you. You don't have to match it.

Money + Trauma Notes

If money was tied to fear, neglect, or control in your past, today's tasks can wake up old pain. Go slower. Pair money steps with regulation steps. Consider trauma-informed therapy, financial counseling, or a trusted mentor. You are not behind. You are healing while learning.

A 4-Week CALM Money Plan

Week 1 - Comfort Focus

- Write 3 self-kind money lines. Read them morning and night.
- Do the Money Story Timeline. Circle one lesson you carry forward.
- Goal: lower shame, tell the truth kindly.

Week 2 - Anchor Focus

- Build your Money Check-In Ritual. Practice twice before you touch numbers.
- Set two weekly money windows. Put them in your calendar.
- Goal: teach your body that money time can be steady.

Week 3 - Look Focus

- Track three money thoughts; flip each one to a balanced line.
- Mute five social accounts that trigger "not enough."
- Goal: shift the story your brain plays on loop.

Week 4 - Move Focus

- Do two 10-minute Money Dates.
- Cancel one subscription or ask for one payment option.
- Start a "calm fund" with whatever you can - $2, $5, $10.
- Goal: build momentum with tiny wins.

Repeat next month. Swap tools as needed. Slow is still forward.

Your Money Crisis Plan (save this in your notes)

If something urgent hits (overdraft, shutoff notice, surprise bill):

1. **Comfort:** "Anyone would feel scared. I can take the next 10 minutes."

2. **Anchor:** 5 slow breaths; feet press into the floor; sip water.
3. **Look:** list the facts (who, how much, by when).
4. **Move:** one call or one email asking for options (payment plan, new due date, fee review).
5. **After:** short walk, light snack, text a support person: "I handled one step."

You don't have to solve it all today. One step reduces harm and builds hope.

Worksheets You Can Use (quick templates)

A. Money Mood Meter (0–10)

- Before task: ____
- Tool used (C/A/L/M): ____
- After task: ____
- Track for two weeks. Look for small drops. That's your nervous system learning.

B. Thought Flip Table

Fearful Thought	Balanced Thought
I'll never get out of this.	This will take time and steps. I can take one today.
I'm bad with money.	I'm learning skills I wasn't taught.
I can't ask for help.	Asking for info is wise and brave.

C. Low-Lift Wins List

Keep a running list of tiny actions that help. Pull one when you freeze.

Reflection: 10 Questions to Ask Yourself

1. What's your earliest memory of money stress?
2. What emotions come up when you check your bank account?
3. What beliefs about money did you grow up with?
4. How does your body react to financial decisions?
5. What kinds of financial situations make you feel most vulnerable?
6. How do you talk to yourself when you feel like you've made a money mistake?
7. Is there a more compassionate way to view your financial habits?
8. What small win around money could you celebrate from this past month?
9. What non-financial resources support your sense of safety?
10. What does financial peace look and feel like for you?

Write or voice-note your answers. No grading. Just the truth.

What I Want You to Carry

Financial anxiety doesn't mean you're failing. It means you care. You care about safety, dignity, and the people you love. You don't have to wait for perfect numbers to feel more grounded. You can build **emotional safety** around money now.

Use **Comfort** to quiet shame.

Use **Anchor** to steady your body.

Use **Look** to tell a fairer story.

Use **Move** to take one tiny step.

You're not behind. You're building. And you're not doing it alone.

CHAPTER TEN

ANXIETY IN THE MODERN WORLD

Life moves fast.

Your phone buzzes.

Your inbox fills up.

The news never ends.

Social media shows everyone's "best day," all day.

So, no surprise, your anxiety feels louder. Your brain wasn't built for non-stop alerts and endless choices. It needs quiet. It needs rhythm. It needs breaks. When it doesn't get those things, your mind stays "on," even when your body is begging for rest.

This chapter is about taking your power back. We'll look at **why** modern life turns the volume up on anxiety and **how** to use the **CALM** Framework - Comfort, Anchor, Look, Move - to feel steadier in a world that never sleeps. Think of this as a friendly guide and a workbook you can use right away.

Why the Modern World Ramps Up Anxiety

1) Technology: the 24/7 connection

Phones, tablets, laptops… they keep you reachable all day and all night. That's useful. It's also draining. Your brain is not a machine. It can't process hundreds of pings without a cost.

- Work emails at 10 p.m.
- Group chats at 2 a.m.

- "One quick scroll" turns into an hour

It's like running a mental marathon without water. You keep going, but your body pays for it - tight shoulders, racing thoughts, sore eyes, and sleep that doesn't refresh you.

2) The news: a constant stream of crisis

Yes, staying informed matters. But hearing about every fire, storm, and conflict - minute by minute - tells your nervous system, "Danger is everywhere." Your body stays in **fight-or-flight** even if the danger isn't near you and there's nothing you can do in that moment.

3) Comparison culture: the highlight reel effect

Online, you see perfect trips, perfect homes, perfect smiles. What you don't see are the bills, the mess, the tears, and the hard talks. When you compare your everyday life to someone else's best moments, you start to feel "less than," even when you're doing fine.

4) Overstimulation: too much, too fast

Notifications. Ads. Multiple tabs. Chores. Messages. The list goes on. When there are too many inputs, your brain gets crowded and jumpy. A crowded brain loves to worry.

A Simple Brain Note

Your brain gives attention to two big things:

- **Threats** (to keep you safe)
- **Rewards** (to keep you engaged)

Breaking news can feel like a threat. Social media can feel like a reward. Put them together with no breaks, and your system gets hooked and tired at the same time. That's the anxiety loop many of us live in now.

Good news: you can change the loop. Not by throwing your phone away, but by using it on *your* terms.

CALM for a Busy, Noisy World

Comfort - be kind to yourself in the noise

- "Of course I feel on edge. This world is loud."
- "I'm not broken for being overwhelmed."
- "I can learn new habits at my own pace."

Shame makes anxiety worse. Compassion softens it. Speak to yourself like you would speak to a friend.

Anchor - make your body feel safe right now

- **Breath reset:** inhale 4, hold 2, exhale 6 (repeat 3–5 times)
- **5-sense check:** 5 things you see, 4 touch, 3 hear, 2 smell, 1 taste
- **Rhythm:** slow walk, gentle sway, shoulder rolls, hand massage
- **Tech pause:** flip your phone face down, or use Do Not Disturb for 20 minutes

Anchors are proof for your nervous system: "We're safe enough to settle."

Look - change the story, not your worth

- **From:** "I have to answer right now."
- **To:** "I'm allowed to respond during work hours."
- **From:** "Everyone else is doing more."
- **To:** "I'm seeing highlights, not the whole story."

- **From:** "If I stop scrolling, I'll miss everything."
- **To:** "I'll choose a news window and get the facts."

When the story changes, your body follows.

Move - take one small, real step

- Turn off three non-urgent notifications.
- Put your charger outside the bedroom.
- Choose two "check times" for news (10 minutes each).
- Replace one scroll session with a short walk or stretch.

Small steps are how your life changes for good.

Practical Tools You Can Use Today

1) The 60-Minute Notification Detox (one-time setup)

Goal: fewer pings, more peace.

- Turn off notifications for social apps and shopping apps.
- Keep alerts for calls, texts from VIPs, calendar, maps, and safety.
- Set **Do Not Disturb** for two focus blocks each day (e.g., 10-12 and 2–3).
- Create a **VIP list** (family, school, caregiver, boss). Only they break through DND.

If you're afraid you'll miss something, try this for 48 hours. You can always add alerts back.

2) The "Two-List" Attention Plan

Draw two columns:

- **Must-See:** calls, texts from VIPs, calendar, banking, health, kids' school

- **Nice-to-See:** news, social, podcasts, hobby channels

Check **Must-See** anytime. Check **Nice-to-See** only during planned windows (e.g., lunch and after dinner for 15 minutes).

3) A Better News Routine

- Pick **one** trusted source.
- Set **two** short windows (AM/PM, 10–15 minutes).
- Ask: "Is there action I can take?" If yes, take it (donate, call, vote). If no, release it with a breath.

4) Sleep-Friendly Phone Setup

- Move your charger **out** of the bedroom.
- Use a $10 alarm clock.
- Set "Wind Down" to auto-dim your phone at a set time.
- Keep a book, journal, or puzzle next to the bed.

Sleep is a superpower for anxiety. Protect it.

5) The 1-Tab Rule (focus at work or school)

- One task = one tab.
- If you must open a new tab, write **why** on a sticky note first.
- When done, close the tab and stand up for 30 seconds.

6) The 20-20-20 Eye and Mind Break

Every 20 minutes, look 20 feet away for 20 seconds.

Add 3 slow breaths.

Your eyes and brain will thank you.

Home Tech Zones (make the rules fit your life)

- **Green Zones (tech welcome):** office, homework desk, living room during set hours
- **Yellow Zones (tech with care):** kitchen table (music okay; no scroll during meals), car (maps okay)
- **Red Zones (tech-free):** dining table during meals, bedroom after lights out, bathrooms (yep)

Post the zones on the fridge. Keep it simple. Keep it kind.

Scripts for Digital Boundaries

At work (late emails):

"Thanks for sending this. I'll review it tomorrow during work hours and reply then."

Group chat (too many pings):

"I'm muting this thread for the afternoon so I can focus. I'll check back later."

Family (bedtime calls):

"I power down at 9 p.m. If it's urgent, call twice. I'll answer."

Yourself (doomscroll urge):

"I'm getting hooked. I'll set a 10-minute timer, then switch to music and stretch."

Short. Clear. Kind. That's enough.

Case Stories (short and real)

Simone, 28 - Doomscroll spiral

Simone wakes up and scrolls for 45 minutes. She feels heavy before her day even starts.

- **Comfort:** "Mornings are hard right now. I'm not bad for coping."
- **Anchor:** Drink water, 3 slow breaths, sunlight for 60 seconds.
- **Look:** "My feed is showing extremes. I'll get facts at noon."
- **Move:** Put phone in the kitchen at night; read two pages in the morning.
- Two weeks later, she still checks her phone—but after water and light. She feels calmer.

Jorge, 41 - After-hours email

Jorge answers messages at 11 p.m. He can't sleep.

- **Comfort:** "I want to be dependable."
- **Anchor:** DND at 8:30 p.m., chamomile tea, box breathing.
- **Look:** "Answering at night hurts my work tomorrow."
- **Move:** Auto-reply after 7 p.m.: "Received—will respond next business day."
- Sleep improves. So does focus.

Amina, 16 - Comparison burn

Amina feels small scrolling "perfect" posts.

- **Comfort:** "It's normal to feel less than when I see highlights."
- **Anchor:** Hand on heart, 5 exhales longer than inhales.
- **Look:** "This is a trailer, not the whole movie."

- **Move:** Mute five accounts that trigger shame; follow three accounts that teach or uplift.
- Her feed feels safer. So does her mood.

Seeing Productivity Differently

Old question: "Did I do enough today?"

New question: "Did I give energy to what matters most today?"

Some days, "what matters" is a big project. Other days, it's calling your grandmother, taking a nap, or cooking a simple meal. Busyness isn't meaning. Rest isn't quitting. Rest is maintenance.

Try this evening check:

- **Win of the day:** one thing you did
- **Care of the day:** one way you supported yourself
- **Next tiny step:** one doable move for tomorrow

That's a kinder scoreboard.

Moving Toward an Intentional Digital Life

Pick 1–2 of these to start:

- Schedule **off hours** each evening (no messages after a set time).
- Unfollow or mute accounts that spike shame, fear, or anger.
- Delete one app you always regret opening.
- Replace one scroll with a body break: walk, stretch, or dance to one song.
- Use "read later" for long articles so you stop skimming 20 tabs.
- Keep devices off the table during meals. Talk, taste, and breathe.

Every intentional choice closes one mental tab. Your brain gets space to think again.

A 7-Day Reset

Day 1: Turn off three non-essential notifications.

Day 2: Create two news windows (AM/PM, 10–15 min).

Day 3: Move your charger out of the bedroom; set DND schedule.

Day 4: Make the Two-List Attention Plan (Must-See / Nice-to-See).

Day 5: Try the 1-Tab Rule for one work block.

Day 6: Tech-free walk for 10 minutes. Notice sounds and light.

Day 7: Review: What helped? What felt hard? Pick one habit to keep.

A 30-Day "Attention Diet" (gentle, realistic)

Weeks 1-2:

- Keep the 7-day habits.
- Add two 20-minute focus blocks daily (DND + one task).
- Unfollow/mute 20 accounts that drain you.

Weeks 3-4:

- Add tech-free hours each weekend.
- Choose a hobby to replace scrolling with (reading, puzzles, gardening, art).
- Share a boundary with one person who will hold you accountable.

Track your sleep, mood, and focus with the SUD scale check each night.

Family, Partners, and Roommates: Make a Technology Use Plan

- **Agree on Red Zones (Where Tech cannot be used):** dinner table, bedrooms after lights out.
- **Agree on Quiet Hours (When you can use tech):** pick a start/stop time for tech use.
- **Plan Alternative Activities to do instead of using Tech:** play a card, go on a walk, dance, stretch break, story time.
- **Repair if you slip:** "We slid back into phones at dinner. Let's try again tomorrow."

Perfection not required. Consistency helps.

Red Flags: Get Extra Support If...

- You feel panicky if you can't check your phone
- You sleep less than 5-6 hours most nights
- Your mood crashes after scrolling
- You can't stop doomscrolling even when it hurts work, school, or relationships
- You feel hopeless, numb, or have thoughts of self-harm

Reach out to a doctor, therapist, or a trusted support line. You matter.

10 Questions to Reflect On

1. How does your phone affect your anxiety?
2. What online habits increase stress for you?
3. What messages do you get from the world about who you should be?
4. What boundaries could help you feel safer online?
5. Can you see productivity differently?

6. What would rest look like today?

7. How can you protect your peace in a loud world?

8. What spaces make you feel calm?

9. What do you want more (and less) of in your daily life?

10. What's one way to move forward with more intention tomorrow?

Takeaway

You can't control the speed of the world. You **can** choose how much of it you let in. Protecting your attention is an act of self-respect. Boundaries are a gift to your nervous system. Pauses are not wasted time, they're fuel.

The calmer your mind, the clearer your life feels. And with **CALM**, Comfort for your heart, Anchors for your body, a new Look at your story, and small Moves you can actually do, you can live on your terms, even in a noisy, busy world.

CHAPTER ELEVEN

ANXIETY DURING LIFE TRANSITIONS

Change, even good change, can shake you.

Your routine shifts. Roles shift. Money shifts. Your sense of who you are can feel wobbly.

So, if your chest gets tight or your mind races during a big life change, you're not broken. You're human.

This chapter is your guide for the messy middle. We'll use **CALM** to walk through common transitions, step by step:

- **Comfort** - name the pain without shame
- **Anchor** - add small moments of safety and predictability
- **Look** - see the story with kinder, clearer eyes
- **Move** - take one small step that builds confidence

You'll find short stories, checklists, scripts, and simple tools you can use today.

Why Transitions Spike Anxiety

- **Your brain loves patterns.** Change breaks patterns, so your inner alarm gets loud.
- **Identity shifts.** "Who am I now?" is a big question. Anxiety shows up to protect you.
- **Loss hides inside change.** Even happy change can include loss: time, money, status, a familiar place, a version of you.
- **Decision fatigue.** Many choices at once tire the brain and body.

Body signs to watch: tight jaw, shallow breath, scattered focus, stomach flips, waking too early, wanting to avoid tasks. These are normal signals. We'll answer them with tools.

A Map for Any Transition

Draw three circles:

- **Control** - your breath, words, schedule, next step
- **Influence** - close people, your team, your doctor, your school
- **Concern** - the big stuff you care about but can't steer alone

Spend most energy in **Control** and **Influence**. Visit **Concern** in short windows.

CALM for Transitions (Quick View)

- **Comfort:** "Change is hard, and it makes sense I feel this."
- **Anchor:** one repeatable ritual in the morning, one at midday, one at night.
- **Look:** ask, "What is ending? What is beginning? What meaning am I adding?"
- **Move:** pick a **10-minute task**. Tiny wins count.

Transitions We'll Cover

- Starting or leaving a job
- Becoming a parent (birth, adoption, foster, blended families)
- Ending a relationship or divorce
- Moving to a new city or country
- Retirement or career shifts
- Health diagnosis or disability
- Starting college or entering adulthood

- Death of a loved one or grief-related change

We'll go deeper into each one with CALM.

1) Starting or Leaving a Job

What it can feel like

Butterflies before emails. Second-guessing every choice. Money worry. "Will I fit in?" or "Who am I if I'm not this job?"

Comfort

- "Nerves mean this matters to me."
- "It's okay to feel grief when I leave a role I knew."

Anchor

- **Pre-email ritual:** feet on floor, inhale 4, hold 2, exhale 6 (x3), then send.
- **Commute cue:** same song or short walk to switch "home → work" or "work → home."
- **Packing cue (leaving):** one box a day; label, close, done.

Look

- Reframe: "I'm not starting from zero. I'm starting from experience."
- "Learning mode is not failing. It's the job of week 1-12."

Move

- Starting:
  - Meet your manager for a 15-minute "first month goals" chat

- o Learn one system a day
- o Ask one helpful person to be your "onboarding buddy"

- Leaving:
  - o Write a 3-line handoff for each project
  - o Update resume/LinkedIn in one sitting
  - o Script for goodbye: "I'm grateful for what I learned. Here's where I'm heading."

Scripts

To manager (new): "What would 'successful first month' look like to you? Top three wins?"

Resignation (brief): "I'm thankful for my time here. My last day will be ___. I'll document my handoffs this week."

2) Becoming a Parent

(Also true for adoption, foster care, step-parenting.)

What it can feel like

Joy and fear at the same time. Sleep loss. Body changes. Role changes. "Am I doing this right?"

Comfort

- "Of course I'm overwhelmed. This is new."
- "Good parents ask for help."

Anchor

- **Two-minute resets:** slow breath while the kettle boils; hand on heart during night feedings.

- **Care circle:** list three people for meals, rides, or sitting with the baby while you shower.
- **Doorway check:** every time you walk through a door, drop your shoulders.

Look

- "Perfect isn't needed. 'Safe enough and loved' is the goal."
- "This season is intense and temporary."

Move

- Ask one person for one specific thing: "Could you bring diapers size __ on Friday?"
- Pick a sleep cue for the home (low light, same lullaby).
- Schedule your own check-in (mood, body, rest) with a provider.

Partner script

- "We're both tired. Can we split nights this week? I'll take midnight–3, you take 3–6."

Case: Maya

She set a 3-item daily list: feed herself, get outside, one load of laundry. Guilt softened. Anxiety dropped.

3) Ending a Relationship or Divorce

What it can feel like

Grief, relief, fear, shame, money strain, paperwork, new housing, "Who am I without us?"

Comfort

- "I can hold sadness and self-respect."
- "My story didn't fail. It changed."

Anchor

- **Home safety:** one cozy corner (lamp, blanket, book).
- **Body reset:** 4–7–8 breaths before tough texts.
- **Support hour:** weekly call with a safe friend or therapist.

Look

- "This is a loss, not a life sentence."
- "Boundaries protect my peace."
- "What values do I want to carry forward?"

Move

- Make a **Separation Checklist:** housing, bank accounts, legal steps, important docs.
- Save all agreements in one folder.
- Co-parent script: "Let's keep messages child-focused and in writing."

Exit script (safety first)

- "I'm not available for conflict. I'll discuss logistics by email on Tuesdays."

Case: Andre

He used calmer channels (email only), blocked midnight calls, and met a lawyer for 30 minutes. Sleep improved.

4) Moving to a New City or Country

What it can feel like

Homesick. Lost. Many tiny decisions. Language and culture stress. "Where do I belong?"

Comfort

- "Missing my old life is love, not weakness."
- "I'm allowed to take it slow."

Anchor

- **Micro-home:** set up a corner first—bed made, lamp, one photo, one plant.
- **Three-block walk:** learn your nearest grocery, pharmacy, and bus stop.
- **Weekly rhythm:** laundry day, market day, call-home day.

Look

- "Every newcomer learns by doing."
- "I can grow roots one hello at a time."

Move

- Join one local group (library class, sport, faith, parent group).
- Learn five phrases you'll use often.
- Map your "care route": clinic, urgent care, best route home at night.

Script for Meeting Neighbors)

- "Hi, I'm __. I just moved in. Any favorite coffee spots nearby?"

5) Retirement or Career Shifts

What it can feel like

Free time that feels too open. Loss of title. Money questions. "Do I still matter?"

Comfort

- "Purpose can look new at this stage."
- "Rest is part of a full life."

Anchor

- **Bookend routine:** morning movement + evening wind-down.
- **Three Ps:** people, place, practice (a person to see, a place to go, a practice to do).

Look

- "Work was one chapter, not the whole book."
- "Curiosity counts as progress."

Move

- Try a 30-day **experiment list**: volunteer shift, short course, mentoring, hobby.
- Money date once a week (10 minutes).
- Write a "legacy line": one sentence about what you want to give now.

Case: Ruth

She missed teaching. She tutored twice a week and joined a walking group. Mood lifted; sleep steadied.

6) Health Diagnosis or Disability

What it can feel like

Fear, anger, relief to finally know, new limits, many appointments.

Comfort

- "My fear makes sense. My body deserves care."
- "I can grieve the old routine and build a new one."

Anchor

- **Appointment ritual:** write 3 questions, bring support, breathe while waiting.
- **Energy budget:** pick 3 things for the day: must-do, want-to, rest.

Look

- "I can ask for plain language."
- "Aids and adaptations are strength, not failure."

Move

- Create a care folder (meds, allergies, providers, emergency contacts).
- Explore supports: PT/OT, peer groups, benefits.
- Tell one trusted person what helps you most.

Script for Medical Provider

- "Please explain in simple steps. What are my top two options and side effects?"

7) Starting College or Entering Adulthood

What it can feel like

Freedom and fear. New systems. New social rules. Money stress. Homesick.

Comfort

- "Firsts feel big. I'm learning."
- "I don't have to know my whole path to take a step."

Anchor

- **Week grid:** classes, food, sleep, study blocks, fun, chores.
- **Home cues:** same mug, same playlist, same Sunday reset.

Look

- "Office hours are for me."
- "Everyone edits their plan. I can too."

Move

- Walk to each class before day one.
- Email a professor: "I'm ___ in your class. I'll attend office hours next week."
- Join one club. Meet one campus support (counseling, advising, tutoring).

Case: Eli

He set two "no-phone study blocks," joined the gaming club, and called home Sundays. Anxiety dropped.

8) Death of a Loved One or Grief-Related Change

What it can feel like

Waves. Fog. Guilt. Relief. Numbness. Panic at night. Big dates are hard.

Comfort

- "There is no right way to grieve."
- "Love and pain can sit together."

Anchor

- **Grief box:** photos, letters, item of theirs, tissue, soft scarf.
- **Breath with tears:** inhale 4, exhale 8; let the body shake and soften.
- Keep meals, meds, and sleep as steady as you can.

Look

- "This is a forever change, and it changes shape."
- "I can carry their love into my next chapter."

Move

- One task a day: a call, a form, a thank-you note, a short walk.
- Plan tough days with a buddy and a script: "I may need to leave early."

- Create a small ritual (light a candle, cook their dish, share a story).

Case: Jonah

He wrote three "letters I never sent." He kept a weekly walk with his cousin. Panic eased.

Decision Fatigue Toolkit

1. Set a **timer for 10 minutes**. Decide or pick a placeholder and revisit tomorrow.
2. Use **two-good-options**: if both are fine, choose the one with less friction.
3. Try the **"later box"**: write down non-urgent choices and choose one time a week to review.

Transition Routine Builder

Morning (5-7 min)

- Comfort line: "Today might feel wobbly. I can be kind to me."
- Anchor: three breaths, water, one stretch.
- Look: "What is one thing that matters today?"
- Move: pick a 10-minute task.

Midday (3-5 min)

- Step outside or to a window. Drop shoulders.
- One body cue: unclench jaw, open hands.

Evening (7-10 min)

- Small tidy or prepare tomorrow's bag.

- Name one win and one care you gave yourself.
- Gentle screen off time (20–30 minutes).

Two-List Method: Loss & Room

- **Loss List:** What is ending? What hurts?
- **Room List:** What might this change make room for?

Write both. Hold both. That's healing.

Permission Slips for Transition (tear-out style)

- I can rest without earning it.
- I can ask for help more than once.
- I can change my mind as I learn.
- I can grieve and still laugh.
- I can start again at any hour of the day.

Tiny Exposure Ladder (if avoidance grows)

Pick a task you fear. Break into 5 steps from easiest to hardest.

Example (calling a clinic):

1. Write the number.
2. Practice the words.
3. Call after hours and leave a test message to yourself.
4. Call and hang up if you panic.
5. Call and book.

Celebrate each rung.

If Panic Hits in the Middle of Change

1. Name it: "This is a panic wave."

2. Sit, feet on floor. Exhale longer than you inhale.
3. Touch five textures in the room.
4. Sip cool water.
5. Say, "Waves rise and fall."
6. When it eases, do one tiny task (text a friend, fold a shirt).

Worksheets (Copy or Print)

A) Transition Snapshot

- What is ending?

  _____

- What is beginning?

  _____

- Biggest fear:

  _____

- Biggest hope:

  _____

- Who are my three helpers?

  _____

B) 30-Day Gentle Plan

- Week 1: stabilize sleep/food/movement
- Week 2: one admin task/day
- Week 3: try one new thing
- Week 4: review + adjust

C) Support Web

- People I can text: _____
- Places that settle me: _____
- Practices that help: _____

D) Energy Budget (Daily)

Must-do: _____ Want-to: _____ Rest: _____

Note how your body feels at night.

Reflection Questions

1. What transition are you currently navigating—or avoiding?
2. What's been hardest about this change?
3. What emotions have you been trying to push away?
4. What makes you feel stable right now, even if it's small?
5. What have you learned about yourself in this transition?
6. What are you proud of so far?
7. What support do you wish you had more of?
8. What past transitions have you survived or grown from?
9. What's one task or conversation that would help you move forward?
10. What permission do you need to give yourself right now?

A Gentle Send-Off

Change brings discomfort. That's okay. You can build steadiness inside the storm.

Use **Comfort** to speak kindly to yourself.

Use **Anchor** to give your body proof of safety.

Use **Look** to name both loss and new room.

Use **Move** to take one small step at a time.

You don't have to do this perfectly. You just have to keep showing up for you.

CHAPTER TWELVE

ANXIETY ACROSS LIFE STAGES

Anxiety isn't one thing for all people. It shifts as your life shifts. The way you felt it in elementary school can look different from high school, work life, parenting, or retirement. Anxiety grows with you. Sometimes it sits quietly in the corner. Sometimes it steps right in front of you and steals the spotlight.

So, here's our plan: we'll look at how anxiety can show up at different ages, why it changes, and how to use **CALM** (Comfort, Anchor, Look, Move) at every stage. I'll keep this clear, caring, and useful. You'll get examples, short scripts, and simple practices. Think of this as a guide you can study and also hand to someone you love.

Why Anxiety Changes Over Time

- **Your brain changes.** As you grow, your brain wiring shifts. Kids feel big feelings but don't yet have strong "brakes." Teens are still building those brakes. Adults have more brakes, but more pressure. Elders may face loss, health changes, or new limits.
- **Your roles change.** School, work, caregiving, parenting, retirement—each role brings new tasks and new worries.
- **Your body changes.** Hormones, sleep, energy, pain, and illness all affect anxiety.
- **Your world changes.** Money, housing, safety, community, culture, and identity shape how safe or stressed you feel.

None of this means you're doing it "wrong." It means you're human.

Anxiety in Childhood (roughly ages 4-10)

Kids rarely say, "I'm anxious." Their bodies speak first. Their behavior speaks second. Words come last.

How it can look

In the body

- Stomachaches before school
- Headaches with no clear cause
- Sweaty palms, fast heartbeat, tight shoulders

In behavior

- Clinging to caregivers
- Refusing school or activities
- Trouble sleeping or nightmares
- Big tears or anger over small changes

Common triggers

- Separation from a parent
- New places or people
- Loud, unpredictable spaces
- Big firsts: first day of school, first sleepover, moving homes

What helps right now

Comfort (what you say)

- "Your feelings make sense."
- "Lots of kids feel this."
- "You're not in trouble for having feelings."

Anchor (what you do)

- "5 things I see" game in the car line
- A "brave buddy" (stuffed animal, smooth rock) to hold
- Count blue cars or count steps to the classroom

Look (how you explain)

- Keep it short and clear: "We're going to the dentist to keep your teeth strong. I'll be right here."
- Draw a simple map: home → dentist → sticker → home

Move (one next step)

- Turn calm into play: jump 20 times, dance for 60 seconds, draw the "worry monster" and give it a silly hat

Tiny scripts

- Child: "I don't want to go!"
- Adult: "Your tummy feels tight because today is new. We can be brave together. Hold my hand. Let's take three slow breaths."

Red flags to notice

- Daily stomachaches for weeks
- Not speaking at school at all (but talking at home)
- Panic-like reactions that block daily life
- If you see these, add more support. Talk with the pediatrician, school counselor, or a child therapist.

Anxiety in the Tween & Teen Years (roughly 11-18)

The teen brain is still wiring the "brakes" (planning, judgment). Feelings feel **big**. The world feels **loud**. Identity questions, grades, social life, body changes, and screens pile on.

How it can look

- Overthinking every text or post
- Fear of judgment in class or sports
- Avoiding events or skipping school
- Comparing themselves to friends, influencers, or celebrities
- Sleep flips: up late, wired-tired, doom-scrolling

What helps right now

Comfort

- "Feeling anxious when life is changing fast is normal."
- "You're learning who you are. That takes time."

Anchor

- "Pre-test ritual": 3 rounds of 4-in/6-out breathing
- Calming playlist in the hallway
- Fidget ring or smooth coin in pocket
- "Phone parking" 30 minutes before bed

Look

- Challenge all-or-nothing: "One grade doesn't define you."
- Swap mind-reading: "You can't know what they think; ask or let it be."

- Values check: "What kind of friend/student/teammate do you want to be today?"

Move

- Small risk, real reward: join a club, ask one question in class, sit with a new person for 5 minutes"Homework in halves": 15 minutes on, short break, repeat

Tiny scripts

- Teen thought: "Everyone will notice if I mess up."
- Reframe: "Most people are busy thinking about themselves. I'll try one sentence."

Family support

- Ask, don't lecture: "On a scale 0–10, how strong is the worry right now?"
- Co-create a plan: "Pick two tools for the morning. I'll help you practice."

Red flags

- Sudden drop in grades, school refusal for weeks
- Self-harm, thoughts of not wanting to live
- Panic attacks that block daily life
- Get help right away. Safety first. You're not alone.

Anxiety in Early & Mid Adulthood (roughly 19-55)

Now the roles stack up: school-to-work, money, dating or parenting, caring for others, career change. Pressure to "have it together" can be heavy.

How it can look

- Overplanning and back-up plans for every plan
- Saying "yes" to avoid letting people down
- Avoiding new roles or projects out of fear
- Racing thoughts at night, busy schedule by day
- Burnout: tired, numb, irritable, checked out

What helps right now

Comfort

- "My worth isn't my to-do list."
- "I'm allowed to be a work in progress."

Anchor

- Morning start: water + 3 breaths before screens
- Midday reset: 5-minute walk, stretch, or sunlight
- Transition cue: music or tea between work and home
- Phone bed: charge your phone outside the bedroom

Look

- Mistake → message: "What did this teach me?"
- Comparison → curiosity: "What do I actually want?"
- "Shoulds" → "Coulds": "I could try this one small step."

Move

- Break projects into **tiny** parts: 15-minute blocks
- Ask for help: share workload, swap tasks
- Practice "good enough" sends: one proofread, then send

Caregiving & parenting notes

- Build micro-rests: 2 minutes of breathing while kids brush teeth
- "Good enough" home routines beat perfect plans
- Repair matters more than perfect: "I got loud. I'm sorry. Let's try again."

Red flags

- Using substances to numb daily
- Panic at work most days
- No joy for weeks
- Reach out: primary care, therapist, support group. Help is not a failure; it's care.

Anxiety in Later Adulthood (roughly 56+)

This stage may bring retirement, health changes, grief, and new limits. It can also bring wisdom, time, and deeper meaning.

How it can look

- Worry about health or mobility
- Restlessness in new places
- Avoiding social events due to energy or fear
- Feeling less in control of choices

What helps right now

Comfort

- "Change is hard. I can be gentle with myself."
- "I've done hard things before."

Anchor

- Daily rhythms: meals, walks, favorite shows, calls with friends
- Gentle movement most days: stretching, tai chi, chair yoga
- Sensory anchors: warm tea, soft blanket, sunshine

Look

- Strength story: "What got me through last time?"
- Focus on what's within reach: "What can I choose today?"

Move

- Social touches: community center, faith group, book club, phone tree
- Purpose sparks: mentor, volunteer, teach a skill
- Health plan: questions for the doctor, notes for meds, steady sleep

Family & caregiver ideas

- Invite, don't push: "Would you like to try the Tuesday group? I'll drive."
- Keep choices simple: "Tea or hot chocolate?"
- Celebrate effort: "I'm proud you went for that short walk."

Red flags

- Weeks of deep sadness, hopelessness, or fear
- Big sleep or appetite shifts
- Thoughts of not wanting to live
- Call the doctor or a crisis line. Your life matters.

Special Transitions Worth Naming

These aren't exact ages, but they often shift anxiety:

1. **College/first job:** leaving home, money stress, new identity

- *CALM:* Comfort ("It's okay to be new"), Anchor (campus map + breathing), Look (one class ≠ whole story), Move (one professor office hour)

2. **Pregnancy/postpartum or new caregiving:** sleep loss, body shifts, new roles

- *CALM:* Comfort ("Hard and precious can both be true"), Anchor (skin-to-skin, slow sway), Look (ask for facts, not fears), Move (accept help; small routines)

3. **Midlife shifts (menopause/andropause, career pivot):** hot flashes, brain fog, identity questions

- *CALM:* Comfort ("My body is changing; I can adapt"), Anchor (cooling breath, fans), Look (reframe "I'm losing it" → "I'm transitioning"), Move (doctor visit, peer group)

4. **Retirement/empty nest:** quiet house, new schedule, purpose search

- *CALM:* Comfort ("Missing them means I love them"), Anchor (new daily rhythm), Look (learn, create, serve), Move (join one group, start one small project)

5. **Grief & medical diagnoses:** fear, scans, caretaking, uncertainty

- *CALM:* Comfort (name the pain), Anchor (one breath, one day), Look (facts + support), Move (appointments, rest, help)

Stage-by-Stage CALM Quick Sheets

Use these like recipe cards.

Kids

- **Comfort:** "Your feelings make sense."
- **Anchor:** Count colors, hold a "brave buddy."
- **Look:** One-sentence plan.
- **Move:** Jump/draw/play for 2 minutes.

Teens

- **Comfort:** "Big change = big feelings."
- **Anchor:** 4–2–6 breaths, playlist, fidget ring.
- **Look:** "One test isn't everything."
- **Move:** One small social or school step.

Adults

- **Comfort:** "I'm more than my output."
- **Anchor:** Morning water + breath, midday walk, phone bed.
- **Look:** Mistake → message.
- **Move:** 15-minute block; ask for help.

Elders

- **Comfort:** "Grace for my changing life."
- **Anchor:** Steady meals, walks, calls.

- **Look:** "I've faced change before."
- **Move:** One connection; one purpose task.

Mini Case Stories (short and real)

Jamal, 9: Won't go to birthday parties.

- *Plan:* Comfort ("New feels big"), Anchor (coin in pocket), Look (schedule: cake at 2, home by 3), Move (stay 30 minutes). Next time: 45 minutes.

Lina, 16: Panic before tests.

- *Plan:* Comfort ("Nerves mean you care"), Anchor (breaths at locker), Look ("One test ≠ me"), Move (ask teacher one question after class).

Marco, 34: Avoids asking for help at work.

- *Plan:* Comfort ("Help is smart"), Anchor (pen grip before meeting), Look ("Sharing load improves quality"), Move (delegate one task this week).

Rosa, 72: Lonely after moving.

- *Plan:* Comfort ("Missing home makes sense"), Anchor (daily tea + porch sun), Look ("I can build new roots"), Move (library book club on Thursdays).

A One-Week Practice Plan for Any Life Stage

- **Day 1:** Write your top 3 triggers for this stage.
- **Day 2:** Pick two **Anchor** tools. Practice when calm.
- **Day 3:** Write three **Comfort** lines that fit you.
- **Day 4:** Catch one anxious thought; do one **Look** reframe.
- **Day 5:** Take one **Move** step (tiny counts).

- **Day 6:** Share your plan with a support person.
- **Day 7:** Celebrate one win; adjust one tool.

Repeat next week with small changes. That's how growth sticks.

10 Questions to Reflect On

6. How did your anxiety look when you were younger?
7. What messages about anxiety did you get growing up?
8. How does your current life stage shape your anxiety today?
9. What do you need at this stage to feel safer?
10. How can you support others in your life with anxiety right now?
11. What would you say to your younger self about anxiety?
12. How have you grown in handling anxious moments?
13. What's one new way you could support yourself this month?
14. How does aging shift your priorities around stress?
15. What legacy do you want to leave around emotional health?

Takeaway

Anxiety wears different faces as life moves. That doesn't make you weak. It makes you human. When you match your tools to your season, using **Comfort** to soften shame, **Anchor** to steady your body, **Look** to shift the story, and **Move** to take one small step, you build a relationship with yourself that lasts. You won't "outgrow" anxiety. You'll **grow with** it, and you'll stay in charge.

CHAPTER THIRTEEN

CAREGIVER ANXIETY

Caregiving is an act of love and often, of overwhelm.

You give rides, meals, time, money, and your energy. You plan, you fix, you remember. You comfort. You keep going. And some days, it feels like you are carrying the sky.

If you're raising kids, helping aging parents, caring for a partner, supporting a friend, or doing all of the above, this chapter is for you. We'll make room for your anxiety and your needs, not just everyone else's. We'll use **CALM** as your steady guide:

- **Comfort** - You're doing more than most people see.
- **Anchor** - Create tiny moments for yourself.
- **Look** - See caregiving as a relationship, not only a task.
- **Move** - Take sustainable steps, not sacrificial ones.

You'll get tools, scripts, checklists, and small plans you can use right away. Keep what helps. Leave the rest.

Why Caregiving Spikes Anxiety

- **Invisible labor.** You remember birthdays, meds, appointments, snacks, forms, rides, moods, and backup plans. Your brain never clocks out.
- **High stakes.** You care about safety, health, school, work, and money. Your alarm system stays "on."
- **Low fuel.** Sleep, food, and movement get last place. Your body runs on empty.

- **Identity pressure.** You feel like you must be strong, kind, patient, and perfect—at the same time.
- **Grief inside care.** Even love can hold loss: lost time, lost energy, lost plans, or lost roles.

What caregiver anxiety can look like

- Body: tight chest, jaw pain, headaches, stomach flips, "wired and tired."
- Thoughts: "I can't drop a single ball," "If I rest, something bad will happen."
- Behavior: over-functioning, people-pleasing, snapping, crying in the car, avoiding hard tasks, doom planning.

You're not failing. Your load is heavy. We'll work with it.

Your Care Map: Control • Influence • Concern

Draw three rings.

- **Control:** your breath, your words, your choices, your schedule, your asks, your boundaries.
- **Influence:** your kids, partner, parents, teachers, doctors, friends, workplace.
- **Concern:** the big picture you care about but can't change alone (systems, waitlists, the past).

Spend most energy in **Control** and **Influence**. Visit **Concern** in **short, planned** windows.

Check-in: Where did I spend my energy today? Where do I want to spend it tomorrow?

CALM for Caregivers (Overview)

- **Comfort:** "It makes sense I feel stretched. I'm carrying a lot."
- **Anchor:** One micro-break morning, one midday, one evening.
- **Look:** "What story am I telling myself about being a 'good' caregiver? Does it help?"
- **Move:** Choose one 10-minute step. Small wins count.

C = Comfort

You're Doing More Than Most People See

Comfort is not "soft". Comfort lowers shame and lowers your alarm. It helps you breathe so you can think.

Normalize your feelings

- "This is hard. I care a lot. Both are true."
- "I can love someone and feel frustrated."
- "Feeling guilty doesn't mean I did something wrong."

Name the invisible labor

Make a quick list of what only *you* track: meds, food, rides, laundry, forms, bedtime, bills, moods, sensory needs, safety checks. Seeing it on paper helps your brain say, "Oh, that is a lot."

Let go of perfectionism as proof of love

Perfection says, "If I mess up, I don't love enough."

Compassion says, "I love deeply, and I'm human. Good enough can be very good."

Comfort scripts

- "I'm one person doing the work of three. I can pace myself."
- "I can choose kindness for me, not just for others."
- "Rest is not selfish. Rest is care for the caregiver."

Good-Enough Caregiver Pledge

I will do what I can, with what I have, in the time I have, and I will call that enough for today.

A = Anchor

Creating Tiny Moments for Yourself

Anchors are short, repeatable resets you can actually keep. Think 30-90 seconds.

Micro-break menu (pick 3 to repeat daily)

- **Doorway exhale:** each time you pass through a door, breathe out long, drop your shoulders.
- **Hand on heart:** 3 slow breaths while you whisper, "Right now, I'm safe."
- **Texture touch:** hold a smooth stone, warm mug, or soft scarf for 60 seconds.
- **Water reset:** drink a full glass. Feel it move down.
- **Sight soothe:** look out a window. Name five colors you see.
- **Song loop:** one song that calms you, once per afternoon.
- **Stretch trio:** neck roll, shoulder roll, forward fold, then roll up slow.
- **60-second step-out:** bathroom door closed, breathe, splash cool water.

Ask your body

"What does my nervous system need right now?"

- If anxious → longer exhales, cool water, press feet into floor.
- If shut down → light movement, fresh air, upbeat song.
- If angry → shake arms/legs, march in place, punch a pillow.
- **Anchors you can use while caregiving**
- During a child's meltdown: soften your jaw, widen your stance, exhale twice as long.
- In a hospital waiting room: feel the chair under you, count your breaths to 10, repeat.
- With dementia "sundowning": lower the lights, play one calm song on repeat, rock gently.
- On hold with offices: stand up, roll your shoulders, sip water, rehearse your ask.

L = Look

From Burden to Bond

Look means you shift the story you tell yourself. You don't lie. You soften sharp edges so you can see your choices.

Common "good caregiver" rules that hurt

- "If I loved them, I wouldn't need a break."
- "I should know what to do all the time."
- "I must keep everyone happy."
- "I have to say yes."

Reframes that help

- "Breaks help me love longer."
- "Learning on the job is still care."
- "I can support feelings. I can't control them."
- "No is a boundary that protects my yes."

Relationship, not only task

Caregiving is not just meds, meals, and rides. It's also presence, humor, stories, and small joys. Tasks matter. Bonding matters too.

Control • Influence • Concern (use it here)

- Control: my tone, my pace, my ask, my rest.
- Influence: daily routines, shared plans, team help.
- Concern: the diagnosis, the waitlist, the past.

Two-Chair Exercise (5 minutes)

- Chair 1: your Inner Critic ("Do more. Do better."). Let it talk for 60 seconds.
- Chair 2: your Inner Caregiver ("I'm doing a lot. I need help."). Answer with kindness.
- Stand. Put your hand on your heart. Choose one sentence to carry forward.

M = Move

Sustainable Steps, Not Sacrificial Ones

We're going for steps you can repeat, not heroic one-time sprints.

Delegate one thing

- Groceries → delivery order once a week.
- Rides → carpool with one neighbor.
- Meals → two "freezer nights" per week.
- Meds → pharmacy auto-refill and text alerts.

Ask for one thing

- "Could you sit with Dad Tuesday 2-4 so I can nap?"
- "Can you be our 'forms person' this month?"
- "Would you do meds pickup on Fridays?"

Say no once

- "I can't do Sunday, but I can do a drop-off Monday morning."
- "I can't host. I can bring paper plates."

Build your care plan

- **Daily:** water, food you can grab, one movement, one anchor, bedtime wind-down.
- **Weekly:** 30-minute block for your money, your schedule, your body.
- **Monthly:** one fun plan that isn't about care (walk with a friend, museum, music).

Respite menu (by time)

- **5 minutes:** stretch, breathe, text a friend, stand in the sun.
- **20 minutes:** nap, walk, shower, chapter of a book.
- **2 hours:** coffee with a friend, movie, long nap.

- **Half day:** nature drive, class, deep clean with music (if that feels good).
- **Full day:** trade coverage with a sibling or friend. Put it on the calendar.

Stoplight tasks

- **Green:** quick wins when tired (dishes, emails, refill pill box).
- **Yellow:** needs a plan (forms, calls).
- **Red:** needs help or a fresh brain (insurance, IEP, legal, finances).

Deep Dives by Care Context

1) Parenting and the Mental Load

What it is

The mental load is the brain work: planning, tracking, remembering, and worrying. It's heavy because it never stops.

Comfort

"I'm carrying the seen and the unseen. That's real."

Anchor

Family "huddle" 10 minutes, twice a week. Same time. Same place. Three questions:

- What's coming up?
- What do we need?
- Who does what?

Look

"I am not the only adult." If there is another adult, share the load on paper. If you are solo, share with a team (family, friends, school, community).

Move

- Make a **Command Center**: calendar, to-do list, inbox tray, pen, sticky notes.
- Teach "pass the baton": "I'm off-duty 7-8 pm. You're on."
- Bedtime rescue: pick **one** of the three: story, bath, or tidy. Not all.

Meltdown plan (for kids)

- **You:** lower your voice, long exhale, soft face.
- **Kid:** space, water, snack, calm corner.
- **After:** name the feeling, practice the skill, move on.

Scripts

- To co-parent: "We need clear jobs. Can we trade bedtime for morning routine this week?"
- To kids: "My body needs a reset. Timer for 3 minutes. Then I'm yours."

2) Elder Care or Serious Illness

Comfort

"Grief can sit beside love. I'm allowed to feel both."

Anchor

- **Appointment bag:** folder, meds list, water, snacks, sweater, phone charger.
- **Waiting room ritual:** breathe 4-2-6, check your questions list, sip water.

Look

"I can ask providers to slow down and use plain words."

"It's okay to get a second opinion."

Move

- **Care binder:** ID, insurance, meds, allergies, providers, diagnoses, advance directives, contacts.
- **Team roles:** driver, meds fill, bill pay, laundry, yard, meals.
- **Home safety:** clear floors, night lights, grab bars, pill organizer, auto-bill pay.

Tough-topic scripts

- Driving: "I love you. I'm worried about safety. Let's talk about other ways to get around."
- Hospital staff: "We need step-by-step instructions and the top two things to watch for at home."

3) Caring for Children with Special Needs

Comfort

"Different needs are not less worthy. My pace can be slower."

Anchor

- Sensory tool kit: noise-reducing headphones, chewies, fidget, weighted lap pad, visual schedule.
- Transition cue: same song or picture card from home → car → school.

Look

"My child's behavior is communication."

"IEP/504 meetings are teamwork meetings."

Move

- Binder: evals, teacher notes, goals, wins, accommodations.
- Email template to school: short, clear, kind, with one ask.
- Sibling care: one-on-one "ten-minute special time."

IEP Meeting Plan

- Write 3 goals.
- Bring support.
- Ask: "How will we measure progress?"
- End with next steps and dates.

4) Sandwich Generation (kids + parents)

Comfort

"I'm pulled both ways. No wonder I'm tired."

Anchor

Color-code the calendar (kids, elders, me). Protect two "me" blocks weekly (even 20 minutes).

Look

"Being needed by many doesn't mean I have to be available to all, all the time."

Move

- Batch errands by location.
- Ask your workplace about flexible options if possible.
- Trade time with a friend ("I'll cover Sunday; you cover next Saturday").

Script

"I can give you 30 minutes Tuesday. I can't do tonight."

5) Emotional Caregiving in Friendships/Partnerships

Comfort

"I can be a safe place and still have limits."

Anchor

Use a **time cap** for heavy talks: "I have 20 minutes now. Do you want to share or do you want help with a plan?"

Look

Supporter ≠ Savior. Ask, "Do you want listening, ideas, or both?"

Move

- Consent to vent: "Is now ok for a heavy topic?"
- Traffic light check-in: red (crisis), yellow (stress), green (ok).
- Aftercare: take a short walk, drink water, stretch.

Compassion Fatigue and Guilt

Signs

Numbness, irritability, dread, no joy, poor sleep, body aches, "What's the point," snapping, tears that won't stop.

Risk is higher when you get little sleep, have few breaks, face long waits, or hold trauma stories.

Care plan

- **Reduce load:** say no once a week; cancel one extra.
- **Increase fuel:** sleep window, real food, water, movement, sunlight.
- **Add joy droplets:** 3 tiny pleasures daily (song, scent, warm drink).

- **Peer debrief:** 10 minutes with a trusted person, not just a screen.
- **Professional support:** therapy, group, or faith leader.

Guilt reframes

- "Guilt is a signal, not a sentence."
- "I can feel guilty and still choose what's sustainable."
- "Saying no now lets me say yes longer."

Your Care Systems (Make it Easy to Keep Going)

Care Circle

List names for rides, meals, errands, sitting, paperwork, tech help, kid swap. Ask *one* clear task per person.

Shared Calendar

One place for meds, visits, school, rides, money dates, your rest blocks.

In-Case Binder & Go-Bag

- Binder: IDs, insurance, meds lists, legal docs, contacts, allergies, recent labs.
- Go-bag: chargers, snacks, water, wipes, sweater, cash, notebook, pen, spare meds.

Script Library

- **Ask for help:** "Could you do __ on __ from __ to __?"
- **Boundary:** "I can't talk about solutions tonight. Let's revisit tomorrow."
- **At work:** "I'm caregiving right now. I can meet deadlines with ____ adjustment."
- **Medical office:** "Please explain in plain words. What are the top two choices?"

Daily, Weekly, Monthly Rhythm (Simple and Real)

Daily 3-3-3

- 3 basics: water • food • sleep cue
- 3 minutes: breathe, stretch, step outside
- 3 wins: two for others, one for you

Weekly Reset (20-30 min)

- Look at the calendar.
- Move one thing off your plate.
- Schedule one joy droplet.
- Pick one admin task and one body task (walk, yoga, nap).

Monthly Check

- What is burning me out?
- What helps the fastest?
- Who can I ask for one thing?

Case Examples

Janelle, single mom of two

She started a Sunday "family huddle," set a 9 pm phone basket, and traded school drop-offs with a neighbor. Her headaches eased.

Marco, caring for his dad with Parkinson's

He built a care binder, set auto-refills, and asked his brother for "laundry duty Fridays." He got his Saturdays back.

Serena, partner with depression

She used time-capped talks, asked for consent before heavy topics, and planned one fun hour a week. Less resentment, more warmth.

Worksheets (Copy/Print)

A) Care Load Inventory

- Tasks only I do:

  _____

- Tasks I can share:

  _____

- Tasks to drop for now:

  _____

B) My Anchor Trio

Morning: _____ Midday: _____ Evening: _____

C) Care Circle Contacts

Rides: _____ Meals: _____ Paperwork: _____ Sits: _____ Tech: _____

D) Stoplight Tasks

Green: _____ Yellow: _____ Red (ask for help): _____

E) Respite Menu

5 min: _____ 20 min: _____ 2 hr: _____ Half day: _____ Full day: _____

F) Body Signal Tracker (7 days)

Signals I felt: _____

Anchors used (C/A/L/M): _____

What helped fastest: _____

Reflection Questions

1. Who are you currently caring for, and in what ways?
2. What's been the hardest part emotionally?
3. What makes you feel most grounded in the middle of caregiving?

4. What unspoken beliefs do you hold about being a "good" caregiver?
5. What do you wish someone would say or do for you right now?
6. What helps you return to yourself after an intense caregiving day?
7. What do you love or value about the person you care for?
8. What does asking for help look like in your world?
9. What story would you tell a friend in your shoes?
10. What does sustainable caregiving look like to you?

CALM Quick Cards

Comfort

- "I'm doing a lot. My feelings make sense."
- "Good enough is still good."

Anchor

- Doorway exhale • Water reset • One-song pause

Look

- "Breaks help me love longer."
- "Supporter, not savior."

Move

- Delegate one task • Ask for one thing • Say one no

A Gentle Send-Off

You hold so much. You hold bodies, schedules, meds, meals, and feelings. You also hold your own heart. You deserve care, too.

Let **Comfort** soften the guilt.

Let **Anchor** steady your body.

Let **Look** widen your view.

Let **Move** make care sustainable.

One breath. One boundary. One small ask.

Repeat. You're building a caregiving life you can live in.

CHAPTER FOURTEEN

HOW TO BE THERE FOR SOMEONE NAVIGATING ANXIETY

When someone you care about is anxious, you might think, "What do I say? What do I do? What if I make it worse?"

Take a breath. You don't have to fix everything. You can **be with** them in a way that brings steadiness.

This chapter gives you a simple, human plan called **CLDS** (sounds like *clouds*). It works with kids, teens, partners, friends, and coworkers. You can use it in person, on the phone, or over text.

CLDS = Comfort • Listen • Destruction/Discharge • Solve

- **C - Comfort:** start with warmth and safety
- **L - Listen:** hold space without fixing
- **D - Destruction/Discharge:** help release built-up energy in safe ways
- **S - Solve:** when they're steadier, pick one next step together

You don't have to use all four. Scan the moment. Choose what fits.

Before You Start: Your Role

- You're a **calm anchor**, not a fixer.
- Ask **consent** before touch or advice.
- Speak **slow, low, and simple**.
- Match your **body** to your words (soft face, open posture, slower breathing).
- Safety first. If there's risk of harm to self or others, get help right away (call your local emergency number or, in the U.S., **988**).

C - Comfort

Goal: help their body feel safer so their brain can settle.

What comfort can look like

- Quiet presence: sit nearby, soften your shoulders, breathe slow.
- Environment shift: lower lights, turn down noise, offer water or a cozy blanket.
- Gentle touch **with consent**: "Do you want a hug or just to sit here together?"
- Grounding words: short, steady, kind.

Scripts

- "I'm here. You don't have to go through this alone."
- "Do you want a hug, a hand to hold, or space next to me?"
- "We can take this minute by minute."

When to use Comfort

- They're tearful, shut down, or shaky.
- They just had a panic surge.
- They say, "I can't talk," or "I don't know."

What not to do

- Don't say "calm down," "it's not a big deal," or "just think positive."
- Don't quiz them with lots of questions.

Tiny tools (60–90 seconds)

- **Hand-to-chest + hand-to-belly** (with consent): "Let's breathe together."
- **Feet press:** "Feel the floor holding you up."
- **Temperature reset:** hold a cool glass or warm mug.

L - Listen

Goal: let them empty out without fixing or judging.

How to listen well

- Give space. Nod. Keep your voice soft.
- Reflect back **feelings**, not facts: "That sounded scary," "You felt cornered."
- Repeat their key words so they feel heard.

Door-openers

- "I'm listening. Say whatever you need to say."
- "Take your time, I'm not going anywhere."
- "Do you want me quiet, or do you want gentle questions?"

When to use Listen

- They've started talking or venting.
- They say, "I just need to get this out."
- They're looping in worry thoughts.

What not to do

- Don't jump to advice, lectures, or your own story.
- Don't argue with their feelings.

Quick reflect phrases

- "You felt blindsided."
- "That brought up a lot at once."
- "You want to feel safe and respected."

D - Destruction / Discharge

(Think: release, not harm.)

Goal: help the nervous system burn off extra energy in **safe** ways.

Why this works

Anxiety often loads the body with "go" energy. Talking isn't always enough. Short bursts of **movement, sound, or force against objects** can open the pressure valve.

Safe options (pick 1–2)

- Rip paper, shred a cardboard box, pop packing bubbles.
- Throw soft items into a laundry basket or against an empty wall.
- Stomp in place, shake out arms, do wall pushups.
- Scream into a pillow or sing loud in the car.
- Sprint to the mailbox and back.
- Dance to one song.
- Towel twist and pull.
- Journal a rage page, then tear it up.

Scripts

- "Do you wanna go outside and yell into the air?"
- "Want to tear some old mail together?"
- "Let's do something that gets this out of your body."

When to use Discharge

- They say, "I'm trapped," "I'm buzzing," "I'm gonna explode."
- They can't sit still; words feel too hard.

Safety notes

- Choose soft or low-risk items.
- Set a short timer (2–5 minutes).
- If you're in public, pick a discreet option (fast walk, bathroom shake-out).

S - Solve

Goal: when they're steadier, **co-create** one small next step.

How to shift into solving

- Ask permission: "Want help with next steps?"
- Keep it tiny: "What would actually help in the next hour?"
- Offer **choices**, not orders: "We could text your boss, eat, or rest first. What feels doable?"

Scripts

- "Let's figure out one next step together."
- "You don't have to fix everything tonight, we can start small."
- "What would make this 10% easier?"

When to use Solve

- Breath and voice are calmer.
- They ask for help.
- They're stuck replaying the same problem.

What not to do

- Don't take over their life.
- Don't make promises you can't keep.

Picking a Starting Point (Quick Scan)

- **C** if they're flooded, shaking, or silent.
- **L** if words are already flowing.
- **D** if the energy is blasting through their body.
- **S** if things have slowed and they want next steps.

You can mix and match: **Comfort + Listen**, or **Discharge + Solve**.

If one step isn't working, slide to another.

Mini Real-Life Scenes

1) Panic surge in public

- **Comfort:** "I'm right here. Let's step outside."
- **Anchor add-on:** feet on the ground, 4-2-6 breath together.
- **Discharge:** hand shake-out for 30 seconds.
- **Solve:** "Want water, a ride home, or five more minutes of fresh air?"

2) 2 A.M. spiral by text

- **Comfort (text):** "I'm here. Breathe with me: in 4, out 6."
- **Listen:** "Type it out. I'll read."
- **Discharge:** "Stand up, stretch shoulders, three slow breaths."
- **Solve:** "One tiny thing - music, tea, or writing a worry on paper for morning?"

3) Teen before a big test

- **Comfort:** "Nerves mean you care."
- **Listen:** "What's the scariest part?"
- **Discharge:** two-minute "shake + jump + breathe" set.
- **Solve:** pick one study card; set a 10-minute timer; snack; lights out by 10.

4) Partner after a harsh meeting

- **Comfort:** blanket, water, quiet.
- **Listen:** reflect feelings, not the office drama.
- **Discharge:** rip junk mail; walk the block together.
- **Solve:** draft one reply line or plan to address it tomorrow.

5) Coworker in a hallway

- **Comfort:** "Want a quiet room for five minutes?"
- **Listen:** "I've got you, talk if you want."
- **Discharge:** wall pushups ×10, slow breath.
- **Solve:** "I can cover your next 15 minutes, sound good?"

Words to Use • Words to Skip

Use

- "I'm here."
- "That was a lot."
- "Your feelings make sense."
- "Minute by minute."
- "What do you need right now?"

Skip

- "Calm down."
- "It's not that bad."
- "You're overreacting."
- "Don't think about it."
- "At least…"

Consent, Culture, and Care

- **Ask first:** "Hug or no hug?"
- Respect **sensory needs** (lights, sounds, smells).
- Honor **identity** and faith practices (prayer, music, language).
- If language is a barrier, slow down and use simple words or text.

Safety Red Flags (Get Help Now)

Call the local emergency number or, in the U.S., **988** for crisis support if you notice:

- Talk of wanting to die, self-harm, or "no reason to live."
- Chest pain, fainting, or breathing trouble that doesn't ease.
- Severe confusion, not knowing who/where they are.
- Violence risk or weapons present.

Stay with them if you can. Keep your voice steady. Help is part of love.

Aftercare For Them

- Water, snack, or warm tea.
- Short rest, shower, or a soft show.
- One gentle win: "You stayed. You breathed. That counts."
- Ask, "Want a check-in tomorrow?"

Aftercare For You (because your nervous system matters too)

- Three slow breaths. Unclench your jaw.
- Shake out your hands. Step outside if you can.
- Name one thing you did well.
- Set a boundary if needed: "I'm logging off for tonight. I'll text you at noon."

CLDS in Different Formats

Three-Minute CLDS

1. **Comfort:** "I'm here." Lower lights, offer water.
2. **Listen:** 60 seconds of quiet listening.
3. **Discharge:** shake-out or paper rip, 60–90 seconds.
4. **Solve:** pick one next step for the next hour.

Text-Only CLDS

- C: "With you. Breathe in 4 and out 6, three times."
- L: "Tell me everything. I'm reading."
- D: "Stand, stretch shoulders; shake hands 20 seconds."
- S: "One tiny next step, music, water, or write it down?"

Pocket Card (say it out loud)

- **C:** I'm here. You're not alone.
- **L:** I'll listen. Take your time.
- **D:** Let's get this out, move, rip, stomp, sing.
- **S:** One small step, together.

Boundaries That Keep Relationships Healthy

- Time box: "I can stay 20 minutes, then I have to leave. I'll text you tomorrow."
- Capacity check: "I love you. I'm at my limit tonight. Can we call your sister or therapist?"
- Team care: help them build a **care circle** so you're not the only support.

Practice Plan (for you)

This week, try:

- One **Comfort** phrase you like.
- One **Listen** line that keeps you quiet.
- One **Discharge** option that fits your space.
- One **Solve** question that invites choice.

Write them on a note in your phone.

Reflection (for supporters)

- Which CLDS step do I use well?
- Which step do I skip when I feel nervous?
- What signals tell me it's time to switch steps?
- What boundary would help me show up longer over time?
- Who is **my** support if I feel drained?

Final Word

You don't need perfect words. You need **presence**.

With **Comfort**, you bring safety.

With **Listen**, you bring dignity.

With **Destruction/Discharge**, you help the body let go.

With **Solve**, you find one small step together.

That's how care feels in hard moments, simple, human, steady.

CHAPTER FIFTEEN

HEALTH ANXIETY (HYPOCHONDRIA)

When your body does something strange, your mind can race.

A new ache. A fast heartbeat. A headline about illness.

Suddenly, every feeling in your body can sound like an alarm.

You're not "too much." You're not broken.

Health-related anxiety comes from care. You want to live. You want to be safe. Your brain is trying to protect you. Sometimes it just gets too loud.

This chapter gives you a clear path to work with that alarm using **CALM**:

- **Comfort** - your worry comes from care
- **Anchor** - reconnect with your present body
- **Look** - shift from catastrophe to curiosity
- **Move** - build health confidence over time

You'll get tools, scripts, and small steps you can use today. Keep what helps. Leave the rest.

How Health Anxiety Works

Your brain has a guard called the **amygdala**. It looks for danger.

Your body has a system called **fight/flight/fawn/freeze**. It helps you act fast.

When you feel a symptom, the guard may shout, "Danger!" even if the symptom is common or mild. Stress hormones rise. Your heart beats faster. Your breath gets shallow. You scan your body for more signs. The scanning itself makes more signs. Now the alarm sounds even louder.

Good news: you can turn the volume down. You can teach your brain to pause, check facts, and respond with care.

Health Anxiety vs. Being Health-Conscious

Health-conscious means you care for your body in steady ways.

Health anxiety means fear runs the show.

Signs you're being health-conscious

- Routine checkups and basic care
- Reasonable questions for your provider
- Choices based on values (sleep, food, movement)
- You can let it go after you act

Signs it's leaning into health anxiety

- Daily body scans, many times a day
- Repeating tests that doctors say you don't need
- Searching symptoms online for hours
- Asking the same question for reassurance again and again
- Avoiding fun or work because you fear a symptom

If you see yourself in the second list, you're not alone. We'll work with it.

Medical Trauma and Fear of Illness

Medical trauma can come from many places: scary procedures, long waits, feeling ignored, bad news, pain that wasn't respected, or watching someone you love get sick. Your nervous system remembers.

What it can look like

- Panic before appointments
- Trouble sleeping the night before a scan

- Fear of hospitals, needles, or tests
- Feeling small or powerless in medical rooms

A gentle truth: your fear makes sense. *Trauma is not drama.* Your body is trying to protect you from more hurt.

Fear of Death or Disability

Many people are scared of loss: of life, health, work, or independence. This fear can sit under health anxiety like a deep drum.

What helps

- Say it out loud: "I'm afraid of dying." or "I'm afraid of losing function."
- Add kindness: "This fear is part of being human."
- Name what matters most to you: time with family, a calm day, faith, service, art, nature
- Let values guide small choices today

We can't remove all risk. We can build a life that feels real and worth living now.

The Google Spiral (Cyberchondria)

You feel a symptom → you search → you find the worst story → your fear rises → you search more. That's the spiral.

Why it sticks

Searching brings short relief ("I'm doing something"). The relief teaches your brain to search again next time. But the relief is short. The fear grows.

We'll replace the spiral with a plan.

Anxiety After a Diagnosis or Health Scare

Even a minor scare can shake you. A new diagnosis can change identity: "Who am I now?" It can bring grief, anger, relief (to finally know), or all three.

Normal reactions

- Feeling hyper-alert to every body change
- Worrying about the future
- Doubting your body

We'll build steadiness while you adjust.

Obsessive Checking and Reassurance-Seeking

Checking and asking can lower fear for a moment. But every time you check "just to be sure," your brain learns: "I must check to be safe." Over time, checking takes more time and joy.

We're going to keep safety. We'll lower the extra checking.

We'll do it gently and step by step.

CALM in Practice

C = Comfort

Your Worry Is Rooted in Care

What to say to yourself

- "My fear is about safety. Of course I feel it."
- "Worry means I care, not that I'm broken."
- "I can be scared and still be kind to me."

Name what your anxiety is trying to protect

- "It's trying to protect my life."
- "It's trying to protect my ability to work."
- "It's trying to protect the people I love from losing me."

Comfort exercises

- **Fear list, then care list:**
- Write three fears (Example: "I'll miss signs of cancer").
- Then write three cares under each fear ("I want to see my kids grow up").
- Put a hand on your heart. Read the care list out loud.
- **Gentle story check:**
- Change "I'm doomed" to "I'm worried because this matters."

Early roots (short reflection)

- "What did I learn about sickness as a child?"
- "Who got sick in my family? What did I see?"
- "How did doctors treat us?"
- These memories shape your body's alarm. Knowing them helps you give yourself more grace.

A = Anchor

Reconnect With the Present Body

When you're anxious, your body can feel like a trap. We will make it feel like a home again, one small step at a time.

Breath tools (pick one)

- **4-2-6 breath:** Inhale 4, hold 2, exhale 6. Repeat 5-7 times.
- **Physiological sigh:** Inhale, quick top-up inhale, long slow exhale. Do 3-5 rounds.
- **Box breath:** Inhale 4, hold 4, exhale 4, hold 4 (if it feels good).

- Touch and movement
- **Grounding press:** Sit. Press feet into the floor. Press palms together. Notice the strength.
- **Temperature shift:** Hold a cool glass or place a warm pack on the chest.
- **Sway and settle:** Stand with soft knees and sway side to side for 30 seconds.

Safe body scan (30-60 seconds)

- Look for **neutral** or **pleasant** spots first (warm hands, strong legs, breath moving).
- Then notice the worried spot with a kind voice: "Hello, tight chest."
- End by returning attention to the neutral spot. This trains your brain to see more than fear.

Create non-anxious wellness rituals

- Drink water when you wake.
- Step outside for light before screens.
- Gentle five-minute stretch before bed.
- Take meds with a simple cue (same song or prayer).
- One "no health content" hour daily (music, craft, nature, comedy).

Medical setting anchors

- Waiting room: breathe 4-2-6, feet on floor, notice 5 things you see.
- During blood draw: hum or count backward by 3s.
- After appointments: stand in the sun or by a window for two minutes before you drive.

L = Look

Shift From Catastrophe to Curiosity

We're not denying risk. We're right-sizing it.

Common thought traps

- If I feel it, it must be dangerous.
- If I don't check, I'm being careless.
- If I had a symptom once, it will come back worse.
- Stories online are the rule, not the rare.

Questions that open space

- "What else could this be besides the worst thing?"
- "Is this new, or has this happened before?"
- "Has any doctor told me a plan? What did they say?"
- "How long would a scary illness take to show? Is this pattern the same?"

Evidence-based reframing (short and kind)

- Catastrophe: "This headache is a brain tumor."
- Curiosity: "Headaches can come from stress, posture, dehydration, or vision. I'll drink water, stretch, and see how I feel in an hour. I can call my provider if needed."

Probability vs. possibility

- Many things are possible. Fewer are likely.
- Ask, "What is most likely today?"

Symptom pie

Draw a circle. Slice possible causes: stress, tension, caffeine, poor sleep, dehydration, posture, infection, side effect, serious illness. Most slices are common. This helps your brain see more than one cause.

Doctor-talk scripts (clear and calm)

- "Here's what I'm feeling, for how long, and what helps or makes it worse."
- "What are the top two likely causes?"
- "What red-flags should make me call you or go in?"
- "If it's not better by ___, what's the next step?"
- "Please explain in simple steps. I get anxious about health."

Write answers down. Take a photo of instructions.

M = Move

Build Health Confidence Over Time

We'll keep safety. We'll cut habits that feed fear.

Reduce checking with gentle limits

- **Delay and decide:** wait 10 minutes before checking. Breathe. Many urges pass.
- **Window it:** one body check in the morning, one in the evening. Not all day.
- **Shrink the time:** if you usually check 20 minutes, try 10.
- **Pick a partner:** tell one trusted person your new plan. Ask them to cheer you on.

Tame the Google spiral

- **Two trusted sources** only (your provider's patient portal, one major medical site).
- **Two search windows** max (10-15 minutes) on planned days.
- No comment threads.
- **Close with care:** stand up, drink water, look out a window for one minute.

Create a whole-person care plan

- **Body:** sleep rhythm, food that fuels, gentle movement, meds as directed.
- **Mind:** CALM steps, therapy if helpful, scheduled "worry time" (10 minutes in the afternoon) so worry has a place and doesn't spread.
- **Support:** one health buddy for rides/calls, one joy buddy for fun.
- **Spirit/values:** faith, nature, art, service—whatever steadies you.

Practice uncertainty in tiny doses

- Skip one check today.
- Wait one hour before searching.
- Drive a familiar route without the "just in case" item you never use (if safe).
- Tell yourself, "I can feel unsure and still be okay right now."

Focus on progress, not certainty

- Track effort, not only outcomes: "I used 4-2-6 breathing," "I delayed checking," "I asked clear questions," "I kept my search window."

Tools, Scripts, and Plans

The 3-Step "Siren Plan" for Scary Symptoms

1. **Comfort:** "This is a fear wave. My body is trying to protect me."
2. **Anchor:** Sit. Feet on floor. 4-2-6 breath ×5. Drink water.
3. Look + Move:
- If you have **red-flag signs** your provider gave you → follow that plan now.

- If not, set a **timer for 60 minutes**. Use your anchor. Recheck. If still worried, use your care plan steps (call nurse line, schedule visit, or rest).

(Ask your provider to help you list red-flags for your condition.)

Appointment Prep Sheet (copy/print)

- Top 3 symptoms (how long, how often, what helps/worsens)
- What I worry it might be (so we can talk about it)
- Top 3 questions
- Meds/supplements list
- "Please explain my plan in simple steps."
- "When do I follow up?" "What are red-flags?"

Take notes. Bring a buddy if you can.

Reassurance Shift: From Asking to Acting

Old loop: ask 5 people → feel better for 5 minutes → fear returns

New loop: use CALM → act on my plan → track my effort

Script for loved ones

- "I'm working on my health anxiety. If I ask the same question again, please say, 'You have a plan. Let's do one step from it.' Then sit with me while I take that step."

Checking Reduction Ladder

Goal: Stop checking my pulse 20 times/day.

1. Wait 2 minutes before the first check.
2. Limit to 10 checks/day for 3 days.
3. Limit to 5 checks/day for 1 week.

4. One morning check + one evening check for 2 weeks.

5. Every other day for 2 weeks.

6. Only when I feel true warning signs **from my doctor's list**.

Celebrate each rung. If you slip, that's okay. Return to the last rung that worked.

Google Rules Card (keep by your computer)

- Two trusted sources.
- Two windows a day, 10–15 minutes max.
- No forums or comments.
- Close with water + window + three breaths.
- If fear spikes: text my buddy, not the search bar.

Case Stories

Aisha - Chest Tightness at Night

Aisha noticed chest tightness after long days. She feared a heart attack. She set a siren plan with her clinic: red-flags to watch, when to call. She added a nightly wind-down: screen off, warm shower, 4-2-6 breath, shoulder stretch. She delayed checking for 10 minutes. Most nights the tightness eased. Her trust rose.

Luis - Post-Scare Spiral

Luis had a scary but minor ER visit. After, he checked his blood pressure many times a day. With his doctor, he made a ladder: 8 checks → 4 → 2 → 1. He moved the cuff to a closet and set two alarms for his chosen times. He used his "Google Rules" card. Within a month, he felt calmer.

Priya - Family Loss and Health Fear

Priya lost her mom to cancer. Every ache felt dangerous. She wrote two lists: Loss (my mom) and Room (I call my aunt each week; I schedule my own screenings; I plant a garden in her honor). She asked her provider for a clear screening schedule. Grief stayed real, and panic softened.

Malcolm - MRI Panic

Malcolm needed an MRI and feared the tube. He practiced anchors at home (box breath + music). At the scan, he brought eye pads and asked for music. He counted sets of 10 breaths. He got through it. Next time felt easier.

Daily CALM for Health Anxiety (10–15 Minutes Total)

Morning (3-4 min)

- Comfort: "Worry tries to help. I can guide it."
- Anchor: 3 slow breaths + water + light.
- Look: "What is the most likely story for my body today?"
- Move: pick one step from my care plan.

Midday (2-3 min)

- Window check (if planned).
- Stand, stretch, step outside. No health content for 10 minutes after.

Evening (5-8 min)

- Gentle movement or stretch.
- Write one worry and one win.
- Screen off 30-60 minutes before bed.
- Sleep cue: same song, prayer, or breath each night.

Worksheets

A) Symptom Pie

Symptom: _____

Possible causes: stress ___ sleep ___ posture ___ food ___ hormones ___ meds ___ infection ___ serious illness ___ other ____

Most likely today: _____

Plan for today (one step): _____

B) My Red-Flag Plan *(ask your provider)*

Red-flags: _____

If yes → where I go / who I call: _____

If no → what I do: _____

C) Worry vs. Action

Worry thought: _____

Kind reframe: _____

One action (or planned inaction): _____

D) Health Confidence Tracker (7 Days)

Efforts I practiced (breath, delay, window, script): _____

How my body felt before / after: _____

One win: _____

Reflection Questions

1. What health fears feel the most present in your life?
2. What early experiences shaped how you feel about illness?
3. What's your relationship with your body when you're anxious?
4. What does your body need when fear kicks in?
5. What beliefs do you hold about what your symptoms mean?
6. What calms you when you're worried about your health?
7. What does it feel like to sit with uncertainty?

8. What health decisions are in your control today?
9. What would self-trust around your health look like?
10. What's one thing you can do this week to care for your health with compassion?

A Gentle Send-Off

Your body is not your enemy. Your worry is not a flaw.

It's care, turned up too high.

Let **Comfort** remind you you're human.

Let **Anchor** teach your body "I'm safe right now."

Let **Look** widen the picture beyond worst-case.

Let **Move** build trust with small, steady steps.

You don't need perfect certainty to live well.

You need a plan you can hold, one breath and one choice at a time.

Chapter Sixteen

Building Resilience

When people hear the word **resilience**, they often picture someone who never bends, never cries, and never asks for help. That picture is a myth. That's acting. Real life is messier and kinder.

Real resilience is **flexible strength**. It bends without breaking. It adapts. It rests, then tries again. It says, "This is hard," and also, "I can take one more step." Some days you stand tall. Some days you sway like a tree in the wind. Your roots hold either way.

You don't need to be unshakable. You need ways to steady yourself when life shakes you.

What Resilience Is (and Isn't)

Not resilience

- Hiding your feelings
- Pushing through no matter the cost
- Pretending you're fine so no one worries

True resilience

- Naming your feelings and telling the truth
- Taking breaks without shame
- Asking for help and accepting care
- Trying again after you rest

Toughness says: "I'm fine."

Resilience says: "I'm struggling, and I will find my way forward."

Exactly. That's the difference.

Why Resilience Matters

Life brings stress, loss, change, and surprise. No one escapes that. Resilience is the skill that helps you:

- Recover after hard moments
- Carry feelings without drowning in them
- Make choices that match your values, even when you're tired
- Keep showing up for yourself

Think of resilience like a muscle. You have it already. You can train it. You can also overuse it and feel sore. Training well means **work + rest + support**.

The Body-and-Brain Side

Think of your body as having a sophisticated alarm system designed to protect you. When this system detects danger—whether real or perceived—it automatically triggers one of four responses: fight, flight, freeze, or fawn. This response is completely normal and has kept humans alive for thousands of years.

Here's what's important to understand: building resilience doesn't mean silencing this alarm system forever. That wouldn't be healthy or even possible. Instead, resilience helps you:

1. Notice the alarm sooner
2. Turn the volume down
3. Choose a useful next step

A helpful idea here is the **window of tolerance**. Inside the window, you feel steady enough to think and act. Outside the window, you feel flooded or numb. Resilience widens your window over time. You do that with practice, support, and gentle wins.

CALM: How Resilience Grows Over Time

Your CALM Framework builds resilience layer by layer.

- **Comfort** - "It's okay to feel this." You lower shame and soften self-attack.
- **Anchor** - "I'm here. I'm safe enough right now." You calm the body.
- **Look** - "What else could be true?" You shift the story.
- **Move** - "One small step." You act in a way that fits your values.

With practice, this becomes more automatic. You'll notice:

- You catch spirals sooner
- You recover faster
- You don't stay stuck as long

The Resilience Ladder

Picture a small ladder you can climb when life feels heavy. Each rung is a doable action.

1. **Name it** - "I feel scared/tired/overwhelmed."
2. **Breathe once** - 4 in, 6 out.
3. **Ground one sense** - touch, sight, sound, smell, or taste.
4. **Speak one kind line** - "I'm having a hard moment, not a hard life."
5. **Choose one value** -courage, care, honesty, rest, faith, growth.
6. **Take one step** - email sent, water sipped, stretch, shower, short walk, ask for help.
7. **Close the loop** - note one win, no matter how small.

When that feels easy, you add a rung. When it feels hard, you step down and rest. That's flexible strength.

Building Your Personal Emotional Toolbox

You don't fix a sink with a hammer. You don't calm a panic with only "positive thinking." You need the right tools for the job. Make four pockets in your toolbox: **Comfort, Anchor, Look, Move**.

Comfort tools (soothe the heart)

- Warm blanket, weighted throw
- Kind self-talk card in your wallet
- Favorite playlist or faith reading
- A photo that reminds you you're loved

Anchor tools (steady the body)

- 4-2-6 breathing (in-hold-out)
- Box breathing (4-4-4-4)
- Cold water on wrists, splash face
- Five-things game: 5 see, 4 touch, 3 hear, 2 smell, 1 taste
- Grounding object (stone, ring, bracelet)

Look tools (shift the story)

- Thought flip sheet (fear on left, kinder truth on right)
- Three questions: "Is this 100% true?" "What's the evidence?" "What would I tell a friend?"
- Values list: "Who do I want to be here?"
- Call or text a wise person

Move tools (tiny action)

- 10-minute tidy, 5-minute walk, 2-minute stretch
- Drink water, eat a snack, take meds
- One email sent; one bill paid; one appointment made
- Shower, fresh clothes, open a window

Note: Your toolbox will change as you change. Swap tools as needed. That's not failure. That's growth.

Myths That Block Resilience (and better truths)

- **Myth:** "If I rest, I'll lose my edge."
- **Truth:** Rest is part of performance. Muscles grow in recovery.
- **Myth:** "If I ask for help, I'm weak."
- **Truth:** Asking for help is a skill. It's wise to share the load.
- **Myth:** "If I feel this pain, I'll drown."
- **Truth:** Feelings rise, peak, and fall. Anchors help you ride the wave.
- **Myth:** "If I'm not perfect, I've failed."
- **Truth:** Progress beats perfection. Small steps compound.

Resilience in Action

The Breakup

Ari's partner leaves suddenly. Sleep is rough. Appetite drops.

- **Comfort:** "Of course this hurts. Loss hurts."
- **Anchor:** 4-2-6 breathing before bed; cold water on wrists in the morning.
- **Look:** "This says something about the relationship, not my worth."
- **Move:** Eat one simple meal, text a friend, 10-minute walk.

- Two weeks later, still sad, but not stuck. That's resilience.

Job Loss

Maya is laid off. Panic, shame, racing thoughts.

- **Comfort:** "I'm not a failure. I'm a person who lost a job."
- **Anchor:** Five-things game when panic spikes.
- **Look:** "What's in my control this week?" (resume, two leads, one rest day)
- **Move:** Schedule unemployment call; update resume 20 minutes a day.
- The storm is real. So is her next step.

Health Scare

Luis is waiting on test results.

- **Comfort:** "Waiting is hard. My fear is a sign I care about my life."
- **Anchor:** Box breathing before sleep.
- **Look:** "Facts, not guesses. I'll list questions for my doctor."
- **Move:** Call clinic to confirm time; walk after lunch; connect with a friend.
- He still worries. He's also functioning. That's flexible strength.

Practicing Resilience Daily

You don't have to wait for a crisis. You can train today.

Daily micro-practices

- One kind sentence to yourself each morning
- Three slow breaths before you check your phone

- One glass of water when you feel wired
- Two minutes of stretching between tasks
- Name one win at bedtime (even "I made the bed")

Weekly rhythm

- One hour of "future care" (meals, bills, meds refills)
- One connection (friend, group, faith, support)
- One unplug block (walk, book, bath, nap)
- One move toward a goal (tiny counts)

Monthly reset

- Review your toolbox. Swap what's stale.
- Pick one value to focus on next month (courage, kindness, honesty, rest).

Repair After Rupture

Everyone snaps or shuts down sometimes. Resilience includes **repair**.

Three-step repair

1. **Own it:** "I got loud. I'm sorry."
2. **Name the why (not as an excuse):** "I was overwhelmed."
3. **Offer a plan:** "I'll step outside next time and come back calmer."

Repair rebuilds trust, with others and with yourself.

Boundaries That Protect Resilience

Boundaries are not walls. They are doors with hinges. You choose when to open and close.

Simple boundary lines

- "I can't take that on right now."
- "Email is best for requests."
- "I'll need to think and get back to you."
- "I'm available until 6 p.m."

Practice saying them out loud. Short and kind is strong.

A 4-Week CALM Resilience Plan

Week 1 - Comfort

- Write three self-kind lines on a card. Read them morning and night.
- Notice one place you add shame. Replace it with one gentle sentence.

Week 2 - Anchor

- Pick two body tools (breath + one sense).
- Practice them daily when you are *not* stressed. Teach your body the path.

Week 3 - Look

- Track one repeating fear. Do a Thought Flip each day (fear → balanced truth).
- Ask one person you trust for a reality check.

Week 4 - Move

- Choose one small courage step tied to your values.
- Do it twice this week. Celebrate with something simple you enjoy.

Repeat the cycle next month with new targets.

Crisis Kit

Pack it now so you don't have to think later.

In your kit

- Note with three breathing patterns
- Two Comfort lines in your handwriting
- Grounding object
- List of two people you can text or call
- Soft snack, water bottle
- A short playlist that calms you
- Safety numbers (therapist, clinic, crisis line in your area)

Put the kit where you can reach it fast (bag, nightstand, desk).

Self-Compassion Scripts

- "This is hard, and I'm doing my best today."
- "I can be kind to myself and still grow."
- "I don't have to earn rest."
- "I can try again after a pause."
- "One step is still a step."

Say them out loud if you can. Hearing your own voice helps.

Measuring Growth Without Being Harsh

Try a simple log:

Three-column check-in

1. **Trigger / stress:** what happened

2. **Tool used:** Comfort / Anchor / Look / Move
3. **Outcome:** 0–10 intensity before and after

Do this three times a week. Over a month, you'll see intensity drop faster or steps happen sooner. That is proof of growth.

When to Get Extra Help

Reach out if you notice:

- Panic most days for weeks
- No joy in things you usually enjoy
- Sleep or appetite far off
- Use of alcohol or drugs to cope
- Thoughts of self-harm or not wanting to live

You deserve care. Support is part of resilience, not the opposite.

10 Questions to Reflect On

1. What does resilience mean to you right now?
2. How do you bounce back after hard moments?
3. How do you comfort yourself after a setback?
4. Which habits help your body feel steady?
5. How have past challenges shaped your strength?
6. When did you reframe a setback and see it differently?
7. What keeps you going when things feel heavy?
8. Which small acts of courage can you celebrate today?
9. What does emotional growth look like in your life this season?
10. What would a resilient version of you do before bedtime tonight?

Takeaway

Resilience isn't about never bending. It's about knowing **how** to bend and **how** to rise. With CALM, you learn to comfort your heart, anchor your body, look at the story with kinder eyes, and move one step at a time. Your toolbox will change. Your seasons will change. Your strength will keep growing.

So, when the wind picks up, you don't have to be a stone. Be a rooted tree. Bend, breathe, and keep your roots. You can make it through this one, too.

BONUS CHAPTER

Anxiety and the 8 Dimensions of Wellness

Anxiety doesn't stay neatly contained in one area of your life. It doesn't politely knock on your emotional door, have a brief visit, and leave everything else untouched. Instead, anxiety has a way of seeping into every corner of your existence—influencing your thoughts, overwhelming your feelings, affecting your physical health, straining your relationships, disrupting your sleep, and even impacting your financial decisions. On difficult days, it can feel like anxiety has taken up permanent residence, leaving you wondering if you'll ever experience lasting relief.

This is precisely where the 8 Dimensions of Wellness become invaluable. Picture them as eight spokes supporting a wagon wheel. When one spoke becomes bent or weakened, the entire wheel begins to wobble, making the journey rough and unstable. However, here's the encouraging truth: strengthening even a single spoke can help stabilize the entire wheel. You don't need to repair every spoke simultaneously—that would be overwhelming and unrealistic. Instead, you can focus on one dimension at a time, and gradually, systematically, your overall well-being becomes more stable and resilient.

These dimensions aren't presented here to add pressure to your already full plate. This approach isn't about achieving perfection or fixing everything at once—that kind of thinking often feeds anxiety rather than healing it. Instead, this framework is about taking manageable steps toward greater balance and gently reminding yourself of an essential truth: you are so much more than your anxious thoughts.

Emotional Wellness

Anxiety loves to tangle itself up with emotions. Sometimes it shows up as fear so sharp it feels like a punch in the chest. Other times, it's guilt - feeling like you should be "handling things better." And sometimes it hides behind anger. (Yes, anger. For many people, especially women of color, anger becomes the "safer" feeling to show than fear or sadness.)

Story: A client I once worked with described it this way: *"It's like my emotions are on a dimmer switch. When anxiety is high, I can't tell if I'm actually sad or mad, if I'm tired or depressed. It all just feels the same - loud and heavy."* When emotions get out of balance, anxiety steps up and everything starts to feel like an emergency.

The brave step is to pause and name what you're actually feeling. It softens the anxiety and instead of saying *"Something is wrong with me,"* you can say *"I'm nervous because this is important to me,"* or *"I feel ashamed because I don't want to let people down."*

Emotional wellness doesn't mean being happy all the time. It means being honest with yourself.

Mini-Practice - The 3-Word Check-In

1. Pause. Put your phone down, close your laptop, or step out of the noise for just a minute.
2. Ask yourself: *If I had to describe how I feel in three words, what would they be?* Don't overthink it. First three words that come to mind are enough.
3. Write them down, or say them out loud. That act alone is powerful.

Over time, you'll notice patterns. Maybe you write "tired" almost every day, or "scared" whenever you have to talk at work. This awareness gives you a way to start addressing the root, instead of drowning in the swirl.

If This Feels Hard: Try using a feelings chart or wheel (many are online). Sometimes anxiety makes it impossible to find the right word. Seeing a list of emotions can unlock something.

Reflection Prompts:

- What emotions do I most often push down or ignore?
- When I say "I'm fine," what do I actually mean?
- How does it feel in my body when I'm being honest about my emotions versus when I'm hiding them?

Physical Wellness

When I ask people where they feel their anxiety, most of them don't point to their heads. They point to their chest, their stomach, their back, their throat. Anxiety may *begin* with thoughts, but it settles into the body like an unwelcome houseguest.

Story: One woman told me that whenever her anxiety was bad, she couldn't eat breakfast. She thought something was wrong with her digestion. But really, her body was in fight-or-flight. Her nervous system had convinced her stomach that she didn't need food—she needed to be "ready to run." That's how sneaky anxiety is.

Your body gives you signals all the time, but most of us are taught to ignore them. In fact, we often do the opposite of what are body is begging for. We drink another cup of coffee when we're exhausted. We stay up late scrolling even though our eyes are burning. We live in bodies that are begging for rest, and then we wonder why our anxiety is screaming.

Physical wellness isn't about forcing your body into some wellness routine that doesn't fit your life. It's about listening. Your body doesn't lie.

Mini-Practice - Temperature Reset

When your anxiety spikes, your nervous system is either revving up (fight/flight) or shutting down (freeze). One of the fastest ways to interrupt that cycle is through temperature.

- Try running cool water over your wrists for 30 seconds.
- Or hold a warm mug in both hands and feel the heat sink into your palms.
- Step outside and notice the air - whether it's humid, crisp, cold, or warm.

That tiny shift is often enough to signal: *"I'm safe right now."*

If This Feels Hard: Your body will often give you cues, so take a minute to pay attention to the cues your body is giving you. Ask yourself: *Where is my anxiety showing up right now?* Naming these feelings, "My shoulders are scrunched up, my stomach's in knots, my teeth are grinding," helps you turn anxiety into awareness.

Reflection Prompts:

- Where in my body does anxiety usually show up first?
- What's one way I can honor my body's signals instead of pushing through them?
- Do I know the difference between "tired" and "burnt out"? How does each feel?

Intellectual Wellness

Anxiety tells you stories. And most of the time, those stories are worst-case scenarios. *"They don't like you." "You'll mess this up." "You can't handle this."* Left unchecked, these stories play on repeat. That's why tending to your intellectual wellness is so important—it gives your mind something else to focus on besides fear.

Story: During the pandemic, one of my clients started doing crossword puzzles. She said, *"It's the only time my brain shuts up."* She wasn't trying to be the best puzzle solver in the world, she was simply giving her mind something else to chew on. That's intellectual wellness.

Curiosity disrupts anxiety. Learning something new or letting yourself play with ideas proves that your mind isn't only a place for worry.

Mini-Practice - Spark List

Take 10 minutes to write a list of things you've always been curious about. They don't have to be "productive." Think:

- Learn how to make dumplings.
- Watch a documentary about whales.
- Try watercolor painting.
- Learn the words to a favorite song in another language.

Circle one thing and take one small step toward it this week. Watch a YouTube video, borrow a book, or buy the supplies. It doesn't matter how small, it matters that you reminded your mind it can stretch and grow.

If This Feels Hard: Anxiety often says, *"You don't have time for that."* If you can't imagine adding something, start tiny. Read one article. Watch a five-minute video. Let your curiosity wake up without the pressure of mastery.

Reflection Prompts:

- What's one subject or hobby that always sparks my interest, even when I'm anxious?
- How do I feel when I let myself play or learn without needing to be perfect?
- Where am I shrinking my curiosity because of fear?

Social Wellness

Anxiety has a way of making you feel like you're on the outside of the party looking through the window. It doesn't matter who you are, most of us know this feeling. You might replay conversations and pick the words used and how you could've phrased things differently, or scroll through social media wondering why you weren't invited out. Sometimes, you might even avoid people altogether because it feels like too much work to connect with them.

Here's the thing: the more you withdraw, the louder anxiety becomes and the harder it becomes to jump back in. Social wellness doesn't mean forcing yourself to be the life of the party. It means find people and places where you find *safe, supportive connections* who see you and and value you just as you are.

Story: I once worked with someone who dreaded going to social gatherings. She would sit in the car rehearsing what to say, then leave early because she felt drained. We shifted her focus from "showing up perfectly" to "finding one safe person." At her next event, she spent most of the evening talking to her cousin in the kitchen. It wasn't flashy, but she left feeling connected instead of exhausted. That's social wellness—quality over quantity.

Mini-Practice - Low-Stakes Reach Out

1. Think of someone you trust. Not necessarily your closest friend, just someone you feel safe with.
2. Send a simple text: "Thinking of you." or "This song reminded me of you."
3. Don't pressure yourself to start a full conversation. The act of reaching out is enough.

This tiny act builds a bridge and reminds your nervous system that you're not isolated.

If This Feels Hard: Try "parallel connection." Sit in the same room with someone you trust while you each do your own thing - watching TV, scrolling, or reading. Presence counts as connection.

Reflection Prompts:

- Who in my life feels safe to be myself around?
- What kind of connection feels nourishing, not draining, to me?
- How do I usually pull away when I'm anxious and what would it look like to reach out instead?

Spiritual Wellness

Anxiety can make you feel like you're floating without a lifejacket. Spiritual wellness is about finding something bigger than yourself to hold onto and finding meaning in whatever you believe or practice. This could be your faith, the values that guide you, or even watching the sunset at night. This gives you a lifejacket when things get rough.

Story: A client once told me she kept a small rock in her pocket. "It reminds me of my grandmother's garden," she said. "Whenever I touch it, I remember I'm part of something bigger than this moment." That's spiritual wellness; it doesn't have to be grand. Sometimes it's as small as a stone in your pocket.

Mini-Practice - One Small Ritual

1. Pick a grounding ritual that fits your life: lighting a candle, saying a short prayer, writing one sentence in a journal, or standing outside for a minute.
2. Do it at the same time each day: morning, before bed, or during a break.
3. Let it signal to your body: "This moment is safe. I am connected."

Rituals don't erase anxiety, but they give you an anchor.

If This Feels Hard: Start by noticing awe. Look up at the sky, listen to birds, or notice the detail in a flower. Awe is one of the quickest ways to tap into spiritual wellness.

Reflection Prompts:

- What helps me feel connected to something bigger than myself?
- Where in my life do I already have rituals, and how do they support me?
- How might awe or gratitude soften my anxiety, even for a moment?

Environmental Wellness

Our surroundings matter more than we admit. A cluttered space can spike anxiety. A noisy or chaotic home can make you feel on edge. Environmental wellness is about creating and visiting places that support calm rather than chaos.

Story: A young mother once shared that her anxiety was worst in the evenings. "Every room feels messy," she said. "I go to bed already overwhelmed." Together, we created a five-minute routine: before bed, she cleared just her nightstand. Not the whole house, just one small space. Over time, that single calm corner became her anchor.

Mini-Practice - One-Thing Shift

1. Look around your environment. Choose one small area that feels chaotic.
2. Spend 5 minutes resetting it. Clear off a surface, open a window, water a plant, or put away a pile.
3. Step back and notice: How does this shift change the way my body feels?

If This Feels Hard: Try "adding calm" instead of decluttering. Place a candle, a soft blanket, or a photo you love in your space. Sometimes adding beauty is easier than removing chaos.

Reflection Prompts:

- What part of my environment increases my anxiety the most?
- Where could I create a small "calm corner"?
- How does my body respond to clutter, noise, or light?

Occupational Wellness

Work consumes the majority of our waking hours, whether it's paid employment, caregiving, volunteering, school, or the general running of a household. Because of the amount of time we devote to working, anxiety often shows up at work. And when work feels overwhelming, unappreciated, or misaligned with your values, you can guarantee anxious thoughts are quick to follow.

Story: One client told me, "My job pays the bills, but every day I feel like I'm disappearing." She wasn't seen for her contributions. Her anxiety was sky-high - not because she hated the work itself, but because the environment drained her spirit. We worked on small boundaries: logging off at her set end time, stepping outside for lunch, saying no to extra unpaid tasks. She couldn't change everything, but those boundaries gave her breathing room.

Mini-Practice - Energy Snapshot

1. At the end of your workday, write two lists: *What drained me today* and *What gave me energy.*
2. Review your lists weekly. Notice patterns - maybe meetings always drain you, while problem-solving gives you energy.
3. Look for one small change. Can you delegate, set a boundary, or protect time for energy-giving tasks?

If This Feels Hard: Start by simply taking two deep breaths before and after work. Mark the transition. Let your body know: *"Work is not my whole life."*

Reflection Prompts:

- Does my daily work add to or lessen my anxiety?
- Where am I tying my worth too closely to productivity?
- What boundaries would help me feel more balanced?

Financial Wellness

Few things stir up anxiety like money does because in American society we don't openly talk about money. Worry about bills, debt, or unexpected expenses (large or small) can keep anyone awake at night. Financial wellness isn't about having it all figured out, it's about acknowledging the issue, identifying what needs to be done, and taking baby steps.

Story: A client once said she never opened her mail because "it always made my chest hurt." Avoidance was her way of coping. We set a tiny goal: open one envelope a week. Over time, she stopped feeling controlled by unopened stacks of paper. Facing her numbers gave her power back.

Mini-Practice – Dollar of Peace

1. Choose a small amount of money - $1, $5, whatever feels possible.
2. Place it in an envelope, jar, or savings account labeled "Peace Fund."
3. This money isn't for bills or emergencies. It's symbolic, proof that you can create security, even in tiny steps.

If This Feels Hard: Practice financial honesty in micro-bursts. Spend 1 minute looking at your bank balance. That's it. Over time, increase by a minute until the fear lessens.

Reflection Prompts:

- What money worries do I avoid because they feel too overwhelming?
- What's one small financial step that would help me feel calmer?
- Do I treat money as a source of shame, or as a tool I can learn to use?

Pulling It All Together

The 8 Dimensions of Wellness remind us anxiety isn't just in your head. Anxiety can show up in all aspects of your life. This might feel burdensome, but it's also freeing because it means you have eight different ways you can start healing.

You don't have to work on them all at once. You don't have to get it perfect. Healing starts with one dimension, one choice, one small act of care.

Maybe today that looks like texting a friend. Tomorrow it could be clearing off your nightstand. Next week, it might be putting $1 in a jar. Each act is a way of telling your anxiety: *"You're here, but you don't get to run my life."*

You are more than your anxiety. You are a whole person, made up of many dimensions. And every dimension deserves care.

Closing Reflection:

Which dimension feels most out of balance in my life right now?

What's one gentle step I can take this week to bring it closer to balance?

CONCLUSION

Carrying CALM Forward

You made it here.

That means you showed up for yourself, again and again.

You learned what anxiety is, how it shows up in your life, and what you can do in the moments that feel heavy. You tried new tools, asked hard questions, and kept going even when parts felt uncomfortable.

That's not small work. That's courage.

Now let's talk about what comes next.

CALM isn't something you "finish." It's not a 30-day sprint, a trend, or a magic button. CALM is a lifelong companion. It walks with you in calm seasons and in messy ones. It sits beside you when you're celebrating. It holds your hand when you're just trying to make it through the day.

Think of CALM like a trusted friend: even if you step away for a bit, you can always return. It will meet you where you are.

The Heart of CALM (one more time)

Comfort - Speak to yourself with care. You are not broken. Your feelings make sense.

Try: "It makes sense that I feel this way right now."

Anchor - Help your body settle in the present.

Try: feet on the floor, three slow breaths, notice a color, a sound, a texture.

Look - Tell a fairer story.

Try: "That didn't go how I wanted, and I can still fix parts of it."

Move - Do one small step that fits your values.

Try: ten minutes on one task, one text for support, one glass of water, one short walk.

Some days you'll move through all four. Other days you'll reach only one. That's still CALM.

Choose Compassion Over Perfection

Perfection says, "If I don't use CALM exactly right, it doesn't count."

Compassion says, "I'm doing the best I can with the tools I have today."

On the days you feel wobbly, compassion is not a reward you earn later. It's the help you need now. Comfort lowers shame. Shame grows anxiety. So, we pick comfort.

Quick compassion lines

- "This is a hard moment. I can be kind to me."
- "I don't have to earn rest."
- "I can learn at my pace."

Trust the Process, Not the Instant Result

You'll use CALM and sometimes things will still feel messy. The talk will still be tense. Your heart will still race before the meeting. Tears may still show up in the car. That doesn't mean CALM failed. It means you're in the middle of the work.

Resilience shows up quietly:

- You bounce back a bit faster.

- Your self-talk softens.
- You feel less stuck and more willing to try again.

Exactly - that's progress.

How to Keep CALM Alive in Daily Life

A. The CALM Daily Rhythm

- **Morning:**
  - *Comfort:* say one kind line out loud.
  - *Anchor:* 3 breaths before screens.
  - *Move:* name one tiny step for the day.

- **Midday:**
  - *Anchor:* stand, stretch, sip water, look out a window.
  - *Look:* ask, "What matters most for the next hour?"

- **Evening:**
  - *Look:* write one lesson from today.
  - *Comfort:* "I did what I could."
  - *Move:* set out one thing for tomorrow (bag by door, outfit, list of three).

B. The CALM Weekly Reset

- Review 1-2 hard moments: Where did you use CALM? Where could you add one step next time?
- Refresh your toolbox: swap one tool that's stale for a new one.
- Plan one connection: friend call, walk, group, faith space.
- Plan one rest block: nap, bath, reading, music, quiet.

C. The CALM Monthly Check-In

- **Three columns:** trigger → tool used → intensity before/after (0–10).
- Spot patterns: What eases you fastest? What drains you?
- Choose a **value of the month** (courage, kindness, honesty, rest, growth) and tie one small action to it.

Your Personal CALM Toolbox (keep it simple)

Comfort (heart)

- Self-kind cue card in wallet
- Warm blanket or scarf
- "Safe person" text template

Anchor (body)

- 4-in / 2-hold / 6-out breathing
- Five-things game (5 see, 4 touch, 3 hear, 2 smell, 1 taste)
- Grounding object (stone, ring, bracelet)

Look (mind)

- Thought Flip sheet: fear on the left, balanced truth on the right
- Three questions: "Is this 100% true?" "What is the evidence?" "What would I tell a friend?"
- Values list: "Who do I want to be here?"

Move (action)

- Ten-minute timer for one task
- Short walk or stretch

- Send one message, make one call, fill one form

Tools should fit **you**. Swap them as your season changes. That's growth, not failure.

Your Rough-Day Plan

(write this in your phone notes)

When anxiety spikes, do:

1. **Comfort:** "This feels big. I can get through the next 2 minutes."
2. **Anchor:** 3 rounds of 4-2-6 breathing; cold water on wrists; feet into the floor.
3. **Look:** name one truer thought: "I'm safe enough right now," or "This is one moment."
4. **Move:** drink water / step outside / text a support person / set a 10-minute timer.
5. **After:** name one win (even tiny) and one tool to try next time.

Keep it where you can see it fast.

How to Measure Growth (without being harsh)

Try a tiny tracker, 3 lines a day:

- **Today's trigger:** _____
- **Tool I used (C/A/L/M):** _____
- **Before/after intensity (0–10):** ___ → ___

Look for trends over 2-4 weeks. Growth often looks like: using a tool sooner, lower "after" number, or quicker recovery.

Common Sticking Points (and gentle shifts)

- **"I forgot to use the tools."**

- *Shift:* Put cues where you look - phone lock screen, sticky notes, bracelet, calendar alerts.
- **"I used CALM and still felt anxious."**
- *Shift:* Anxiety may not vanish, but it can soften. Aim for "safer and steadier," not "perfectly calm."
- **"I guilt myself for resting."**
- *Shift:* Rest is maintenance. Rest keeps your tools working.
- **"I want to quit when I slip."**
- *Shift:* Slips are part of learning. Repair beats perfect. Start again with one small step.

Your CALM Scripts

Comfort

- "I'm having a hard moment, not a hard life."
- "My feelings are valid, even when they're loud."

Anchor

- "In for 4, hold for 2, out for 6."
- "What do my feet feel like on the floor?"

Look

- "What else could be true right now?"
- "If a friend felt this, what would I say?"

Move

- "What's the next 10-minute step?"
- "Who can I ask for support?"

A 30-Day CALM Maintenance Plan

Week 1 - Comfort Focus

- Write 3 self-kind lines. Read them morning and night.
- Catch one self-attack each day; swap it for a kinder line.

Week 2 - Anchor Focus

- Practice 4-2-6 breathing twice a day when you are calm.
- Add one body cue before stress (stand, stretch, sip water).

Week 3 - Look Focus

- Do one Thought Flip per day. Keep them in a note on your phone.
- Ask one trusted person for a reality check this week.

Week 4 - Move Focus

- Choose one value-based goal. Break it into tiny steps.
- Do two tiny steps this week. Celebrate both.

Repeat next month with new lines, new tools, and one new goal.

Your Resource Shelf

- **CALM Framework** summary sheet (keep in your bag)
- **Worksheets** from each chapter (print or keep as phone PDFs)
- **Reflection prompts** for journaling or voice notes
- **Crisis kit** list (contacts, meds list, grounding steps)
- **Support list** (therapist, doctor, two trusted people, local warmline)

If some pages aren't filled out yet, no rush. They're tools, not homework.

Your Next Steps (pick one)

- Focus on **one** CALM step this week.
- Use the **matching worksheet** to make it real.
- Track what helps and what doesn't.
- Adjust without shame.

Tiny changes, layered with time, turn into a new way of living.

A Note on Getting Extra Help

Reach out if you notice: panic most days, no joy for weeks, big changes in sleep or appetite, using alcohol or drugs to numb, or thoughts of self-harm. Care is available. You deserve it.

A Letter You Can Read on Hard Days

Hey you,

If you're reading this, today is heavy. You don't have to handle the whole day at once. Try the next 2 minutes. Put your feet down. Breathe 4-2-6. Drink water. Text one person. You've lived through hard things before. You're allowed to rest. You're allowed to ask for help. One small step is still a step. I'm proud of you for showing up.

What I Want You to Carry With You

Anxiety is not your enemy. It's a signal. It wants to keep you safe, even when it goes too far. CALM is your way to listen without losing yourself.

You built awareness.

You gathered tools.

You practiced compassion.

Now you get to carry CALM into your mornings, your relationships, your work, your rest, and your dreams. You don't have to do it perfectly. You just have to keep showing up for yourself.

So, take a breath.

Pick one small step.

Let's keep going, together.

STAYING CONNECTED

Thank you for walking through this journey with me.

Every page, reflection, and breath you've taken is proof that healing doesn't have to be loud to be real.

You've learned to notice your anxiety with compassion,

to ground yourself when things get loud,

and to move forward in small, kind steps.

That's progress that matters.

Your story doesn't end here.

I'd love to stay connected as you keep growing, resting,

and reclaiming calm in your everyday life.

For more resources, tools, and encouragement, follow along:

LinkedIn	Facebook	Instagram

You'll find short videos, weekly practices, and new ways to keep using what you learned in these pages.

GO DEEPER

If you'd like more guided support, explore the **Reclaiming C.A.L.M. Online Companion Guide.**

You'll find expanded exercises, printable tools,

and step-by-step practices to keep your momentum going.

Simply scan the QR code below to access it:

Remember:

You're never walking this road alone.

Keep showing up for yourself – one breath, one thought,

one gentle move at a time.

I'm cheering you on every step of the way.

With care,

Whitney

REFERENCES

American Psychiatric Association. (2022). *Diagnostic and statistical manual of mental disorders* (5th ed., text rev.). American Psychiatric Publishing.

Barlow, D. H. (2002). *Anxiety and its disorders: The nature and treatment of anxiety and panic* (2nd ed.). Guilford Press.

Beck, J. S. (2020). *Cognitive behavior therapy: Basics and beyond* (3rd ed.). Guilford Press.

Beck, A. T., & Clark, D. A. (1997). An information processing model of anxiety: Automatic and strategic processes. *Behaviour Research and Therapy, 35*(1), 49–58.

Borkovec, T. D., & Roemer, L. (1995). Perceived functions of worry among generalized anxiety disorder subjects: Distraction from more emotionally distressing topics? *Behavior Therapy, 26*(5), 777–792.

Brown, R. P., & Gerbarg, P. L. (2005). Sudarshan Kriya yogic breathing in the treatment of stress, anxiety, and depression: Part II—Clinical applications and guidelines. *The Journal of Alternative and Complementary Medicine, 11*(4), 711–717.

Buhr, K., & Dugas, M. J. (2002). The Intolerance of Uncertainty Scale: Psychometric properties of the English version. *Journal of Anxiety Disorders, 16*(1), 65–80.

Carleton, R. N. (2016). Into the unknown: A review and synthesis of contemporary models involving uncertainty. *Journal of Anxiety Disorders, 39*, 30–43.

Clark, D. A., & Beck, A. T. (2010). *Cognitive therapy of anxiety disorders: Science and practice.* Guilford Press.

Clark, D. M., & Wells, A. (1995). A cognitive model of social phobia. In R. G. Heimberg, M. R. Liebowitz, D. A. Hope, & F. R. Schneier (Eds.), *Social phobia: Diagnosis, assessment, and treatment* (pp. 69–93). Guilford Press.

Craig, A. D. (2002). How do you feel? Interoception: The sense of the physiological condition of the body. *Nature Reviews Neuroscience, 3*(8), 655–666.

Craske, M. G., Treanor, M., Conway, C. C., Zbozinek, T., & Vervliet, B. (2014). Maximizing exposure therapy: An inhibitory learning approach. *Behaviour Research and Therapy, 58*, 10–23.

Dugas, M. J., & Robichaud, M. (2007). *Cognitive-behavioral treatment for generalized anxiety disorder: From science to practice.* Routledge.

Duhigg, C. (2012). *The power of habit: Why we do what we do in life and business.* Random House.

Edmondson, A. C. (2018). *The fearless organization: Creating psychological safety in the workplace for learning, innovation, and growth.* Wiley.

Figley, C. R. (Ed.). (1995). *Compassion fatigue: Coping with secondary traumatic stress disorder in those who treat the traumatized.* Brunner/Mazel.

Foa, E. B., & Kozak, M. J. (1986). Emotional processing of fear: Exposure to corrective information. *Psychological Bulletin, 99*(1), 20–35.

Foa, E. B., Hembree, E. A., & Rothbaum, B. O. (2007). *Prolonged exposure therapy for PTSD: Emotional processing of traumatic experiences.* Oxford University Press.

Guilbert, P., & Neff, K. D. (2018). *The mindful self-compassion workbook.* Guilford Press.

(Also see: Neff, K. D. (2011). Self-compassion. William Morrow.)

Hayes, S. C., Strosahl, K. D., & Wilson, K. G. (2012). *Acceptance and commitment therapy: The process and practice of mindful change* (2nd ed.). Guilford Press.

(See also: Hayes, S. C. (2019). A liberated mind. Avery.)

Heimberg, R. G., & Becker, R. E. (2002). *Cognitive-behavioral group therapy for social phobia: Basic mechanisms and clinical strategies.* Guilford Press.

Hofmann, S. G., Asnaani, A., Vonk, I. J., Sawyer, A. T., & Fang, A. (2012). The efficacy of cognitive behavioral therapy: A review of meta-analyses. *Cognitive Therapy and Research, 36*(5), 427–440.

Hofmann, S. G., Sawyer, A. T., Witt, A. A., & Oh, D. (2010). The effect of mindfulness-based therapy on anxiety and depression: A meta-analytic review. *Journal of Consulting and Clinical Psychology, 78*(2), 169–183.

Kabat-Zinn, J. (2013). *Full catastrophe living* (Rev. ed.). Bantam.

Kanter, J. W., Manos, R. C., Bowe, W. M., Baruch, D. E., Busch, A. M., & Rusch, L. C. (2010). What is behavioral activation? A review of the empirical literature. *Clinical Psychology Review, 30*(6), 608–620.

LeDoux, J. E. (1996). *The emotional brain: The mysterious underpinnings of emotional life.* Simon & Schuster.

Lehrer, P. M., & Gevirtz, R. (2014). Heart rate variability biofeedback: How and why does it work? *Frontiers in Psychology, 5,* 756.

Linehan, M. M. (2015). *DBT skills training manual* (2nd ed.). Guilford Press.

Maslach, C., & Leiter, M. P. (2016). Understanding the burnout experience: Recent research and its implications for psychiatry. *World Psychiatry, 15*(2), 103–111.

(See also: Maslach, C., & Leiter, M. P. (2022). The burnout challenge. Harvard Business Review Press.)

McEwen, B. S. (1998). Protective and damaging effects of stress mediators. *New England Journal of Medicine, 338*(3), 171–179.

Neff, K. D. (2003). Self-compassion: An alternative conceptualization of a healthy attitude toward oneself. *Self and Identity, 2*(2), 85–101.

Nolen-Hoeksema, S. (2000). The role of rumination in depressive disorders and mixed anxiety–depressive symptoms. *Journal of Abnormal Psychology, 109*(3), 504–511.

Ogden, P., Minton, K., & Pain, C. (2006). *Trauma and the body: A sensorimotor approach to psychotherapy.* W. W. Norton.

Porges, S. W. (2011). *The polyvagal theory: Neurophysiological foundations of emotions, attachment, communication, and self-regulation.* W. W. Norton.

Primack, B. A., Shensa, A., Sidani, J. E., et al. (2017). Social media use and perceived social isolation among young adults in the U.S. *American Journal of Preventive Medicine, 53*(1), 1–8.

Rapee, R. M., & Heimberg, R. G. (1997). A cognitive-behavioral model of anxiety in social phobia. *Behaviour Research and Therapy, 35*(8), 741–756.

Sapolsky, R. M. (2004). *Why zebras don't get ulcers* (3rd ed.). Henry Holt.

Salkovskis, P. M. (1991). The importance of behaviour in the maintenance of anxiety and panic: A cognitive account. *Behavioural and Cognitive Psychotherapy, 19*(1), 6–19.

Siegel, D. J. (2012). *The developing mind* (2nd ed.). Guilford Press.

(See also: Siegel, D. J. (2010). Mindsight. Bantam.)

van der Kolk, B. A. (2014). *The body keeps the score: Brain, mind, and body in the healing of trauma.* Viking.

Warwick, H. M. C., & Salkovskis, P. M. (1990). Hypochondriasis. *Behaviour Research and Therapy, 28*(2), 105–117.

World Health Organization. (2019). *International classification of diseases for mortality and morbidity statistics* (11th rev.). WHO.

Zarit, S. H., Reever, K. E., & Bach-Peterson, J. (1980). Relatives of the impaired elderly: Correlates of feelings of burden. *The Gerontologist, 20*(6), 649–655.

www.ingramcontent.com/pod-product-compliance
Lightning Source LLC
Chambersburg PA
CBHW070912130626
46555CB00001B/107